Career-Specific English for Airline Service and Travel

Airline Service and Travel English

Kim, Young-Mi
– Bachelor's Degree in English Language and Literature: The Catholic University of Korea
– Master's Degree in TESOL: Pennsylvania State University, USA
– PhD in English Language: Inha University, Korea
– English Professor in the Department of Airline Service Management, Inha Technical College, Korea

Son, Ki-Pyo
– Bachelor's Degree in English Language and Literature
– Master's Degree in American Literature
– PhD in American Literature: Ajou University, Korea
– English Professor in the Department of Tourism English, Ansan College, Korea

Airline Service and Travel English

Authors Kim Young-mi, Son Ki-pyo
Publisher Chung Kyu-do
Editors Lee Jeong-eun, Kim Tae-yeon
Designers Kim Seong-hee, Yun Hyeon-ju

Stock images shutterstock.com
Logos of airlines wikipedia.org

First Published December 29, 2017
By Darakwon, Inc.
Darakwon Bldg., 211, Munbal-ro, Paju-si, Gyeonggi-do 10881
Republic of Korea

Tel 82-2-736-2031 (Ext. 552)

Copyright © 2017 Kim Young-mi, Son Ki-pyo
All rights reserved. No part of this publication may be reproduced, stored in a retrieval system, or transmitted in any form or by any means, electronic, mechanical, photocopying
or otherwise, without the prior consent of the copyright owner. Refund after purchase is possible
only according to the company regulations. Contact the above telephone number for
any inquiries. Consumer damages caused by loss, damage, etc. can be compensated according
to the consumer dispute resolution standards announced by the Korea Fair Trade
Commission. An incorrectly collated book will be exchanged.

ISBN 978-89-277-0956-5 13740
http://www.darakwon.co.kr
Main Book / Free MP3 Available Online
12 11 10 9 8 7 6   24 25 26 27 28

Contents

Unit	Title	Page
01	When Would You Like to Travel?	8
02	May I See Your Ticket and Passport, Please?	16
03	Would You Like a Window or Aisle Seat?	24
04	Welcome Aboard!	32
05	Would You Like Something to Drink?	40
06	What's the Purpose of Your Visit?	48
07	My Baggage Is Missing	56
08	I'd Like a Double Room with an Ocean View	64
09	We Have a Business Center on the Second Floor	72
10	What Kinds of Cars Do You Have?	80
11	Are You Ready to Order?	88
12	I Need a Present for My Parents	96
13	I Want to See Some Sights in New York	104

Listening Script   112

Answer Key   128

Plan of Book

Unit	Topics	Goals	Listening
01 When Would You Like to Travel?	• Flight Reservations • Classes of Seats	• How to reserve flight tickets • How to read times, dates, and phone numbers • The names of international airlines	• Canceling a Reservation • Calling about a Reservation • Special Meal Requests • Purchasing a Ticket
02 May I See Your Ticket and Passport, Please?	• Flight Check-In • Excess Baggage Charges	• How to check in • How to tell time • How to say numbers	• Passengers with Special Needs • Passports • Mileage Upgrades • Standby Passengers
03 Would you Like a Window or Aisle Seat?	• Seat Assignments • Security Screening	• How to assign a seat • How to give directions • How to go through a security check	• Location of Lounges • Pre-Boarding Announcement • Security Screening • Pre-Check-In Seat Assignment
04 Welcome Aboard!	• Boarding • Reading Material Service	• How to get information from the flight information board • How to guide passengers on board • The items onboard commercial airplanes	• Seatbelts • Separated Passengers • Changing Seats • Lavatory Information
05 Would You Like Something to Drink?	• Meal Service • In-Flight Duty-Free Sales	• How to request in-flight meals • How to buy duty-free items • How to fill out entry cards	• Coffee Service • Meal Service • Passenger Requests • Handling a Sick Passenger
06 What's the Purpose of Your Visit?	• Immigration • Customs Inspection	• How to communicate at immigration and customs • How to use the quantifiers *much* and *many* • About facilities in international airports	• Immigration Inspection • Transit Passenger Information • Terminal Information • Customs Inspection
07 My Baggage Is Missing	• Lost and Found • Baggage Claim	• How to claim and find your lost baggage • How to fill out a property irregularity report form • How to describe the shapes and colors of your property	• Baggage Claim Information • Delayed Baggage • Lost Baggage • Baggage Complaints

Unit	Topics	Goals	Listening
08 I'd Like a Double Room with an Ocean View	• Hotel Reservation • Hotel Check-In	• Types of accommodations and hotel rooms • How to reserve a hotel room • How to check in at a hotel	• No Rooms Available • Changing Your Reservation • Smoking or Nonsmoking? • Different Room Rates
09 We Have a Business Center on the Second Floor	• Complaints and Requests • Checking Out	• Various kinds of hotel services • How to request and complain about hotel services • How to check out	• Guest Room Equipment • Making Complaints about Hotel Rooms • Asking to Keep Baggage • Correcting Mistakes
10 What Kinds of Cars Do You Have?	• Renting a Car • Getting Lost in the City	• How to rent a car • How to ask for and give directions • The classes and types of cars • Road signs	• Making a Reservation • Gasoline Charge • Giving Directions • Asking for Directions
11 Are You Ready to Order?	• Being Seated and Served • Ordering Meals	• The different types of restaurants • Various foods on menus • How to order meals and to make complaints • How to pay the bill	• Visiting a Restaurant • The Way a Steak Is Cooked • Mistaken Orders • Checking a Bill
12 I Need a Present for My Parents	• Buying at a Clothing Store • Getting a Refund	• About shopping places • How to get help from a sales clerk • How to ask about goods in different sizes, styles, and colors • How to get a refund	• Price Bargaining • Asking for Information • Getting Help from a Sales Clerk • Payment Methods
13 I Want to See Some Sights in New York	• A Trip to the Statue of Liberty • Helicopter Tour	• How to describe and recommend tourist attractions • How to ask for information about sightseeing • About various tourist attractions	• Admission Fees • Asking Strangers for a Favor • Visiting a Museum • Ticket Reservations

Unit 01 When Would You Like to Travel?

In this unit, you will learn:
1. How to reserve flight tickets
2. How to read times, dates, and phone numbers
3. The names of international airlines

Warm-Up

A Look at the following world map. Ask and answer the questions with your partner.

- Do you like traveling?
- Yes, I do. / No, I don't.
- Where would you like to travel to?
- I would like to travel to _____.
- Have you ever traveled to any foreign countries?
- Yes, I have. I visited _____. / No, I haven't.

B Look at the corporate logos of some international airlines. Ask and answer the questions with your partner.

- What international airlines do you know?
- I know _____.
- What airline would you like to fly on?
- I'd like to fly on _____.

Vocabulary

Complete the following sentences by using the words from the box.

| airfare | available | confirm | departure | destination |
| passengers | prefer | request | reservation | round-trip |

1 There is a delay in the _____ of our plane.

2 I'd like to book a _____ ticket, please.

3 Tickets are still _____ for Friday, May 11.

4 I'd like to _____ my reservation on Flight 723.

5 What is the cheapest _____ from Seoul to Chicago?

6 Can I change my _____ to a different date?

7 New York is a popular tourist _____ in America.

8 I _____ Singapore Airlines because of its excellent service.

9 All _____ must have a valid passport and other travel documents at all times.

10 Passengers can _____ a special meal 24 hours prior to their flight's departure time.

Listen Up

Listen to the dialogue and choose T (true) or F (false).

		T	F
1	The passenger is going to New York.	☐	☐
2	The passenger wishes to travel on Thursday, March 15.	☐	☐
3	The passenger prefers a business-class seat.	☐	☐
4	Flight KA023 departs at 7:00 PM.	☐	☐
5	The passenger's reservation number is 797-1234.	☐	☐

Let's Talk ❶ Listen to the conversation and practice it with your partner.

Flight Reservations

Agent Good morning. Koreana Air reservations. Jiyoon Lee speaking. How may I help you?

Passenger I'd like to reserve a round-trip ticket from Seoul to New York.

Agent Okay. When would you like to travel, sir?

Passenger I'd like to leave on June 15 and return on July 1. Are there any seats available?

Agent One moment, please. Let me check for you. Thank you for waiting, sir. How many people will be traveling?

Passenger I am traveling by myself.

Role-Play

Practice the conversation with your partner again. Use the ideas in the box.

A Good morning. ❶_____ reservations.
   ____(Your Name)____ speaking. How may I help you?

B I'd like to reserve a round-trip ticket from Seoul to ❷_____.

A Okay. When would you like to travel, sir/ma'am?

B I'd like to leave on ❸_____ and return on ❹_____.
   Are there any seats available?

A One moment, please. Let me check for you.
   Thank you for waiting, sir/ma'am. How many people will be traveling?

B I am traveling by myself.

❶ Airline	❷ Destination	❸ Departure	❹ Arrival
Delta Airlines	Los Angeles	January 21	January 29
Asiana Airlines	Paris	February 2	February 12
Air China	Shanghai	August 23	August 30
Korean Air	Rome	September 14	September 22
ANA	Tokyo	October 5	October 15
Cathay Pacific Airways	Hong Kong	November 16	December 7

Language Practice

A When are the special days below? Ask and answer questions with your partner.

> A When is ___your birthday___ ?
> B It's on _____.

birthday

Valentine's Day

Arbor Day

Buddha's Birthday

Memorial Day

Hangul Proclamation Day

B Work with your partner. Take turns asking and answering the following questions.

> A What is the most important day of the year for you?
> B It's Christmas. It's on December 25 every year.
> A What do you do on that day?
> B I go to church and spend lots of time with my family.

A What is the most important day of the year for you?
B It's _____. It's on _____.
A What do you do on that day?
B I _____.

Let's Talk 2

Listen to the conversation and practice it with your partner. 01-03

Classes of Seats

Agent   What class would you prefer?

Passenger   I'd like to reserve a seat in business class.

Agent   All right. May I have your name, please?

Passenger   My name is Peter Philips.

Agent   Could you spell your last name as it's written on your passport?

Passenger   Sure. P-H-I-L-I-P-S.

Agent   Thank you. Could I get your contact number in Korea, please?

Passenger   Sure. My business number is 202-555-0165.

Agent   Thank you very much for your cooperation.

Role-Play

Practice the conversation with your partner again. Use the ideas in the box.

A   What class would you prefer?

B   I'd like to reserve a seat in ❶_____.

A   All right. May I have your name, please?

B   My name is ❷_____.

A   Could you spell your last name as it's written on your passport?

B   Sure. ❷_____.

A   Thank you. Could I get your contact number in Korea, please?

B   Sure. My business number is ❸_____.

A   Thank you very much for your cooperation.

❶ Class	❷ Name	❸ Contact Number
first class	Henry Gray	415-367-3124
prestige class	Ruby Hall	408-239-5937
economy class	Lisa Kelly	510-797-4321
business class	Debra Johnson	605-897-3545
premium economy	Jason Rodriguez	778-660-3434

12 Unit 01

Language Practice

A Complete each dialogue by using the correct word or phrase from the box.

| name | credit card | address | signature | contact number |

1. **A** May I have your _____, please?
   B Sure. Where should I sign?

2. **A** May I have your _____, please?
   B My address is 530 Linden Road, University Park, PA 16802.

3. **A** May I have your _____, please?
   B I am Michael Hopkins. That's H-O-P-K-I-N-S.

4. **A** May I have your _____, please?
   B Sure. Here you are.

5. **A** May I have your _____, please?
   B It's 415-973-1461.

B Work in pairs. Ask and answer the following questions with your partner.

1. **A** What airline do you prefer to fly with?
   B I prefer _____.

2. **A** What colors do you prefer?
   B I prefer _____.

3. **A** What sport do you prefer?
   B I prefer _____.

4. **A** What class do you prefer to take?
   B I prefer _____.

5. **A** Which season do you prefer?
   B I prefer _____.

a. soccer

b. English class

c. *Koreana Air*

d. red and white

e. winter

Practice More

A Listen to the dialogue. Then, complete the following script. 🔊 01-04

Canceling a Reservation

Agent — Good morning. Koreana Air Reservations. How may I help you?

Passenger — I'd like to ¹_____ my reservation on Flight 823 on the ²_____ of this month.

Agent — Sure. May I have your name, sir?

Passenger — Tom Clause. C-L-A-U-S-E.

Agent — One ³_____, please, Mr. Clause... Thank you for waiting. Your reservation is now ⁴_____.

B Listen to the dialogue. Then, answer the following questions. 🔊 01-05

Calling about a Reservation

1 Why did the passenger call?

2 Where is the passenger going?

3 When is the passenger going to leave?

C Listen to the dialogue. Then, put the following sentences in the correct order. 🔊 01-06

Special Meal Requests

1. I have requested a vegetarian meal for you.
2. Certainly. May I have your reservation number, please?
3. It's 953598.
4. Just a minute, please. Thank you for waiting.
5. Is it possible to request a vegetarian meal?

D Listen to the dialogue. Then, choose T (true) or F (false). 🔊 01-07

Purchasing a Ticket	T	F
1 The passenger made a reservation last month.		
2 The passenger wants to cancel his reservation.		
3 The passenger is going to Jakarta.		
4 The passenger wants to pay by credit card.		

Wrap-Up

A Complete the sentences with the words or expressions you used in this unit.

| available | cash | contact number | check | confirmed |
| cooperation | flight | make a reservation | prefer | traveling |

1. I'd like to _____ for a flight to L.A.
2. Could I get your _____ in Korea, please?
3. What class would you _____?
4. Are there any seats _____?
5. How many people will be _____?
6. How will you be paying? Will that be _____ or credit card?
7. Let me _____ for you.
8. You are now _____ on Flight KA738 to Chicago on April 5.
9. I need to change my _____ to May 7.
10. Thank you very much for your _____.

B Look at the airline e-ticket. Then, answer the following questions.

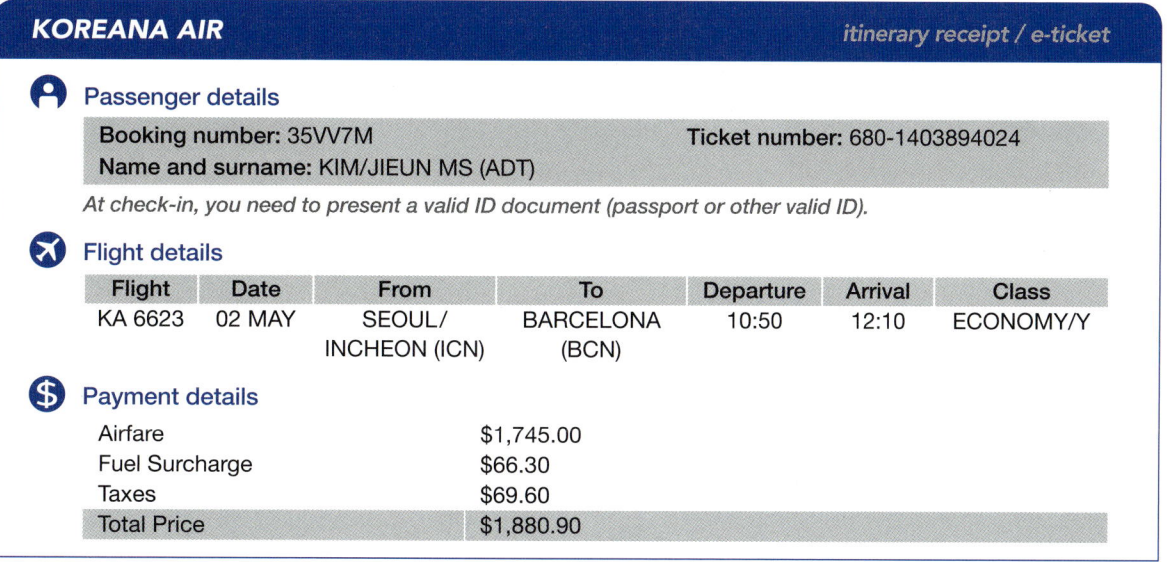

1. Is this a round-trip or one-way ticket?
2. What's the e-ticket number?
3. What airline is the passenger using?
4. What time does the passenger depart from Incheon?
5. How much did the passenger pay for this ticket?

Unit 02
May I See Your Ticket and Passport, Please?

In this unit, you will learn:
1 How to check in
2 How to tell time
3 How to say numbers

Warm-Up

A Look at the following pictures. Then, match the pictures with the correct words in the box.

| passport | conveyor | visa |
| kiosk | baggage tag | suitcase |

1
2
3
4
5
6

B Ask and answer the questions with your partner.

- Do you have a passport? — Yes, I do. / No, I don't.
- What is your passport number? — It's JR1256041.
- When does your passport expire? — It expires on January 19, 2023.
- Do I need a visa to visit the United States? — Yes, you do. / No, you don't need one.

Vocabulary

Complete the following sentences by using the words from the box.

baggage claim	restricted	check	delay	excess
expiration	prohibited	carry-on	scale	stopover

1 Smoking is strictly _____ anywhere on the plane.

2 Passengers can collect their bags at the _____ area.

3 The _____ date on his passport is in two years.

4 I weighed myself on the _____.

5 There will be a _____ in the departure of planes bound for Chicago.

6 Passengers will also be able to _____ their luggage at Seoul Station.

7 Last year, around 2.1 million people used Incheon Airport as a _____.

8 If your luggage exceeds these limitations, you will be asked to pay an _____ baggage fee.

9 Most airlines allow you to bring one _____ bag.

10 Passengers need to have some information about _____ items on flights.

Listen Up

Listen to the three check-in announcements and choose T (true) or F (false).

		T	F
1	Check-in service has been stopped due to heavy snow.	☐	☐
2	Koreana Air Flight 211 to Canada has been canceled.	☐	☐
3	The new departure time is 10:30.	☐	☐
4	Baggage security is now taking a short time.	☐	☐
5	Passengers can proceed to the departure lounge immediately after they check their bags.	☐	☐

Let's Talk 1

Listen to the conversation and practice it with your partner. 🔊 02-02

Flight Check-In

Agent	Good morning, sir. May I see your ticket and passport, please?
Passenger	Here you are.
Agent	Thank you. You are going to New York.
Passenger	Yes. Is the flight going to depart on time?
Agent	Yes, sir. The departure time is 10:40 AM. Do you have any baggage to check in?
Passenger	Yes, I have two suitcases.
Agent	Would you please put them on the scale?
Passenger	Sure.

Role-Play

Practice the conversation with your partner again. Use the ideas in the box.

A Good morning, sir. May I see your ticket and passport, please?

B Here you are.

A Thank you. You are going to ❶_____.

B Yes. Is the flight going to depart on time?

A Yes, sir. The departure time is ❷_____. Do you have any baggage to check in?

B Yes, I have ❸_____.

A Would you please put it/them on the scale?

B Sure.

❶ Destination	❷ Time	❸ Baggage
Beijing	7:50 PM	three suitcases
Prague	9:30 AM	one bag and two boxes
Athens	11:20 PM	five boxes
Istanbul	1:15 PM	one golf bag
Honolulu	3:40 PM	one bicycle

Language Practice

A Use each city's name in the underlined parts. Then, practice using the different time zones by using the clocks.

- **A** You are flying from <u>Seoul</u> to <u>Sydney</u>, right?
- **B** Yes, the flight takes several hours.
- **A** Right. But what about the time change? Aren't they in different time zones?
- **B** Actually, <u>Sydney</u> is <u>one hour ahead</u> of <u>Seoul</u>.
- **A** Oh, I didn't realize that.
- **B** I have to fly from <u>Seoul</u> to <u>Bangkok</u> next week.
- **A** <u>Bangkok</u> is <u>two hours behind</u> <u>Seoul</u>.

B The following are items prohibited on airplanes. Read the list and mark them from the pictures.

Prohibited Items

Explosives and flammable items such as matches and lighters
Flammable gases such as butane gas and spray cans
Flammable liquids such as gasoline and paint
Radioactive, infectious, and toxic substances such as chlorine, oxidizers, mercury, and radioactive materials
Other dangerous items such as weapons, sharp objects, fire extinguishers, and tear gas

May I See Your Ticket and Passport, Please? 19

Let's Talk 2

Listen to the conversation and practice it with your partner. 02-03

Excess Baggage Charges

Agent Excuse me, sir. You are going to New York via Tokyo. Are you aware of this, sir?

Passenger Yes, I am. Can you through-check my bags to New York?

Agent No problem, but your baggage is over the weight limit.

Passenger Oh, really? Well, can't you just check them anyway?

Agent I'm sorry, sir, but I have to charge you for the excess weight.

Passenger Well, how much is that going to be?

Agent It will be 200 U.S. dollars or 226,200 Korean won.

Passenger Wow, that's quite expensive!

Role-Play

Practice the conversation with your partner again. Use the ideas in the box.

A Excuse me, sir. You are going to ❶_____. Are you aware of this, sir?

B Yes, I am. Can you through-check my bag(s) to ❶_____?

A No problem, but ❷_____.

B Oh, really? Well, can't you just check it/them anyway?

A I'm sorry, sir, but ❸_____.

B Well, how much is that going to be?

A It will be 200 U.S. dollars or 226,200 Korean won.

B Wow, that's quite expensive!

❶ Destination & Stopover	❷ Baggage Problem	❸ Solution
Barcelona via Frankfurt	your baggage is too big	you can check in two bags
Dubrovnik via Istanbul	only 2 pieces of baggage are allowed	I have to charge you for the excess piece
Dubai via Hong Kong	each bag must not weigh more than 32kg	you must pay for the extra weight

Language Practice

A Practice saying the following prices with your partner.

lollipop	lipstick	perfume	watch	camera	tablet PC
₩1,467	₩25,000	₩382,645	₩209,000	₩1,635,800	₩370,000

A How much did you pay for _____?

B _____ won.

B Read the following information about carry-on baggage and choose T (true) or F (false).

Carry-On Baggage

Carry-on items are highly restricted in terms of items and liquids. It is suggested that you take your valuables, handbags, and personal items in your carry-on while leaving all other contents in your checked baggage.

It is also highly recommended that you take your valuables and fragile items with you as carry-on items.

Normally, carry-on baggage should have smaller dimensions than 55x40x20cm, and the sum of the three dimensions should not exceed 115cm while weighing no more than 10 to 12 kilograms. However, 1 additional female handbag, purse, baby food, baby basket, or small briefcase is allowed as a carry-on item.

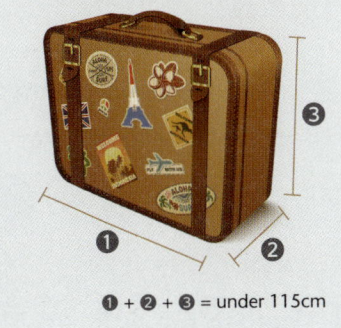

❶ + ❷ + ❸ = under 115cm

	T	F
1 Passengers have to leave their jewelry and cameras in their checked baggage.	☐	☐
2 Passengers had better take fragile items in their carry-on baggage.	☐	☐
3 Passengers can hand-carry baggage which weighs 15 kilograms.	☐	☐

Practice More

A Listen to the dialogue. Then, complete the following script. 🔊 02-04

Passengers with Special Needs

Passenger	I asked one of your ¹_____ agents to assist me at the airport.
Agent	Sure. What is your name and ²_____?
Passenger	My name is Christina Aguilera. I'm on Flight KA706.
Agent	One moment, please. Miss Aguilera, a wheelchair is ³_____ for you. Our agent will help you get ⁴_____.

B Listen to the dialogue. Then, answer the following questions. 🔊 02-05

Passports

1 Where is the passenger going?
2 What is the problem?
3 What does the passenger have to do?

C Listen to the dialogue. Then, put the following sentences in the correct order. 🔊 02-06

Mileage Upgrades

1. May I have your SKYPASS card, please?
2. Oh, I don't have it with me.
3. Thank you. Within Southeast Asia, you need 15,000 miles to upgrade a round-trip ticket not during the peak season.
4. April 10, 1987.
5. I would like to use some of my miles to get an upgrade from economy to prestige class.
6. Don't worry, sir. May I have your date of birth?

D Listen to the dialogue. Then, choose T (true) or F (false). 🔊 02-07

Standby Passengers

	T	F
1 The passenger doesn't want to take the next flight.		
2 The passenger is going to Nagoya.		
3 An MCO is a compensation voucher.		
4 This dialogue takes place on the phone.		

Wrap-Up

A Complete the sentences with the words or expressions you used in this unit.

| aware | check | excess | get an upgrade | may |
| need | on time | scale | through-check | weight limit |

1 _____ I see your ticket and passport, please?
2 Is the flight going to depart _____?
3 Do you have any baggage to _____?
4 Would you please put them on the _____?
5 Are you _____ of this, sir?
6 Can you _____ my bags to New York?
7 Your baggage is over the _____.
8 I have to charge you for the _____ weight.
9 You _____ 15,000 miles for a free return ticket.
10 I would like to use some of my miles to _____ from economy to prestige class.

B The notice has some information about restricted items on flights. Read the notice and answer each question.

Restrictions on Liquids, Gels, and Aerosols in Carry-On Bags

- Passengers must carry all liquids in containers smaller than 100ml. These containers must fit in a 1-liter transparent, re-sealable plastic bag.
- Passengers may only carry one plastic bag each. Passengers must put all containers bigger than 100ml in their checked luggage, or airport security may take and destroy them.
- Medication and baby food for use during the flight may be in containers bigger than 100ml.

1 What should passengers do with containers with more than 100ml of a liquid?
2 What can passengers do with containers with less than 100ml of a liquid?
3 What items bigger than 100ml can people carry on flights?

Unit 03
Would You Like a Window or Aisle Seat?

In this unit, you will learn:
1. How to assign a seat
2. How to give directions
3. How to go through a security check

Warm-Up

Look at the seat map of a plane. Then, talk with your partner about the seats that you prefer.

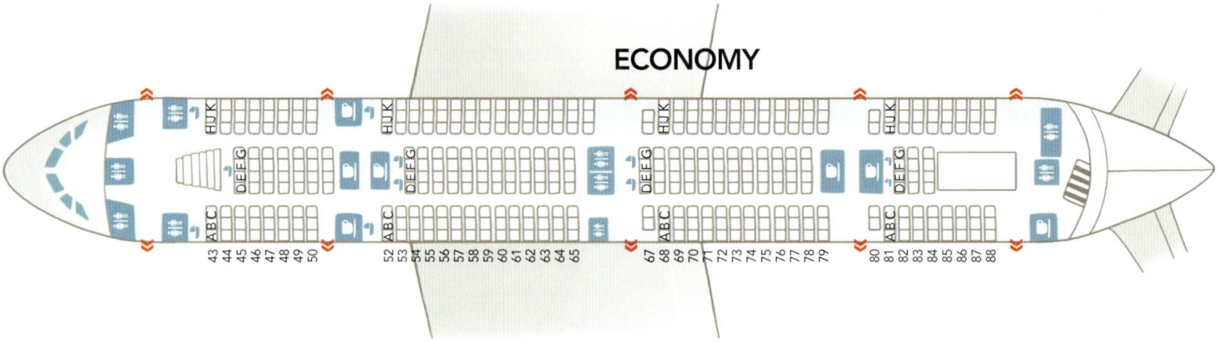

ECONOMY

- Emergency Exit
- Galley
- Lavatory
- Closet
- Bassinet

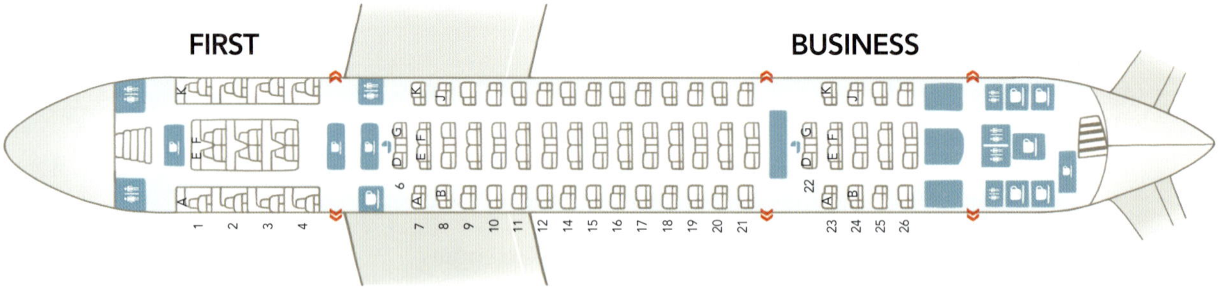

FIRST   BUSINESS

> Where do you want to be seated?

> Which seats do you prefer?

> I want to be seated in _____.

> I think _____ are good because _____.

Vocabulary

Complete the following sentences by using the words from the box.

aisle	assignment	cabin	board	currency
detector	immigration	proceed to	security	upstairs

1 The emergency exits are located on both sides of the _____.

2 _____ and safety are two major concerns at international airports.

3 Please raise your arms to the sides while the metal _____ is running on your body.

4 I always choose an _____ seat because I don't enjoy looking out the window.

5 Passengers with disabilities are allowed to _____ before other passengers.

6 She visited the _____ office to renew her visa.

7 Check the exchange rate before you change your foreign _____.

8 You must go through a security screening before you _____ your boarding gate.

9 If the flight is overbooked, you may not get a seat _____.

10 Please think about your neighbors who live _____ as well as downstairs.

Listen Up

Listen to the dialogue and choose T (true) or F (false). 03-01

                                                                           T   F

1 The passenger is going to Los Angeles. ☐ ☐

2 The departure time is 10:40 AM. ☐ ☐

3 The passenger prefers an aisle seat. ☐ ☐

4 The passenger has three suitcases. ☐ ☐

5 The Member's Club Lounge is on the third floor. ☐ ☐

Let's Talk ❶ Listen to the conversation and practice it with your partner. 🔊 03-02

Seat Assignments

Agent   Would you like a window or aisle seat?

Passenger   Do you have a seat by the emergency exit?

Agent   One moment, please. Are you traveling with anyone?

Passenger   No, just me.

Agent   Okay, your seat number is 12C. You'll be boarding from Gate 23 at 8:30 AM.

Passenger   Thank you. Oh, where is a convenience store?

Agent   There's one on the second floor. Thank you for flying on Koreana Air. Have a nice trip.

Passenger   Thank you very much.

Role-Play

Practice the conversation with your partner again. Use the ideas in the box.

A   Would you like a window or aisle seat?

B   Do you have ❶_____?

A   One moment, please. Are you traveling with anyone?

B   No, just me.

A   Okay, your seat number is 12C. You'll be boarding from Gate 23 at 8:30 AM.

B   Thank you. Oh, where is ❷_____?

A   There's one ❸_____. Thank you for flying on Koreana Air. Have a nice trip.

B   Thank you very much.

❶ Seat	❷ Place	❸ Location
a window seat	a pharmacy	downstairs
an aisle seat	an Internet cafe	on the second floor
a middle seat	a currency exchange counter	on the right
a seat by the emergency exit	a duty-free shop	on the corner
a seat with legroom	a mobile phone rental office	on the left

Language Practice

A Complete the following conversations by using the correct words from the box. Then, practice the conversations with your partner. (Some words may be used more than once.)

| on the first floor | on the second floor | across from |
| next to | between | in front of |

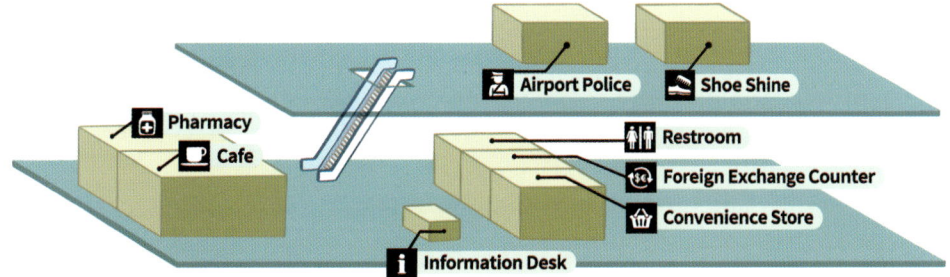

1 Q Excuse me. Where is the pharmacy?
  A It's located ___on the first floor___. It's ___across from___ the restroom.

2 Q Excuse me. Where is the airport police?
  A It's located _____. It's _____ the shoe shine.

3 Q Excuse me. Where is the information desk?
  A It's located _____. It's _____ the convenience store.

4 Q Excuse me. Where is the foreign exchange counter?
  A It's located _____. It's _____ the restroom and the convenience store.

B Look at the boarding pass. Then, answer the questions.

1 What is Flight KR113's destination?
2 What time does Flight KR113 depart?
3 What gate does Flight KR113 leave from?
4 What time does Flight KR113 start boarding?

KOREANA AIR

NAME KIM/MIYOUNGMS
FROM SEOUL
TO   NEW YORK

FLIGHT	DATE	DEPARTURE TIME
KR113	24JUN	17:30
GATE	BOARDING TIME	SEAT
11	17:00	50G

Let's Talk ❷

Listen to the conversation and practice it with your partner.

Security Screening

Security Personnel	May I see your passport, please?
Passenger	Here you go.
Security Personnel	Thank you. Would you please put your carry-on bag through the X-ray machine?
Passenger	Sure. Do I have to take off my jacket?
Security Personnel	Yes. And please put your laptop computer in the security bin.
Passenger	Okay. Can I carry this bottled water?
Security Personnel	No, you can't. Please proceed through the metal detector.
Passenger	All right. I'll have to throw away this water first.

Role-Play

Practice the conversation with your partner again. Use the ideas in the box.

A   May I see your passport, please?

B   Here you go.

A   Thank you. Would you please put your
    ❶_____ through the X-ray machine?

B   Sure. Do I have to take off my ❷_____?

A   Yes. And please put your ❸_____ in the security bin.

B   Okay. Can I carry this bottled water?

A   No, you can't. Please proceed through the metal detector.

B   All right. I'll have to throw away this water first.

❶ Carry-On Item	❷ Clothing	❸ Belonging
backpack	belt	wallet
box	shoes	coins
stroller	cap	cellular phone
violin	coat	keys

28 Unit 03

Language Practice

A Match each question with the appropriate response in the box.

1. Is there a laptop computer in your bag? _____
2. Do you have any coins in your pockets? _____
3. Would you please open your handbag, miss? _____
4. Would you please raise your arms to the sides? _____
5. Would you please place your bag through the X-ray machine again? _____

> a. Do I have to take it out?
> b. Do you need to recheck it?
> c. Certainly. Is this high enough?
> d. What's the problem with my bag?
> e. Oh, I'm sorry. I forgot to take them out.

B Read the information on the fast track service pass below. Then, choose the passengers who can have this service.

Fast Track Service Pass

Passengers with this pass (may be accompanied with 3 companions) may enter through Fast Track (1, 6) or the side doors near departure gates 2~5.

Hours of Operation
Fast Track: 07:00~19:00
Side doors: Please refer to the hours of operation of each departure gate.

Date _____._____._____.
No. of companions ☐ 0 ☐ 1 ☐ 2 ☐ 3

1
2
3
4
5

Practice More

A Listen to the dialogue. Then, complete the following script. 🔊 03-04

Location of Lounges

Passenger   Excuse me. Where is the Morning Calm Lounge?

Agent   It's ¹_____ on the third floor. Just take the escalator on your left and then ²_____. The signs will guide you.

Passenger   Where can I find the ³_____ lounge?

Agent   You can take the elevator at the ⁴_____ of the hall on the left to the ⁵_____ floor. The lounge will be on your left.

B Listen to the dialogue. Then, answer the following questions. 🔊 03-05

Pre-Boarding Announcement

1. Where is this flight going?
2. What does the speak mention?
3. What is the new boarding time?

C Listen to the dialogue. Then, put the following sentences in the correct order. 🔊 03-06

Security Screening

1. Oh, really? Let me open it for you to check.
2. I'm afraid that your handbag contains an item that is not allowed on the flight.
3. Is there a problem?
4. Excuse me, ma'am. Would you please open your handbag?
5. Thank you, ma'am. This hand lotion is 180ml. You may return to the check-in counter and put it in your checked baggage. Otherwise, we need to confiscate it.

D Listen to the dialogue. Then, choose T (true) or F (false). 🔊 03-07

Pre-Check-In Seat Assignment	T	F
1 The passenger wants to be assigned a seat.		
2 The passenger's reservation number is 1172-7771.		
3 The seat the passenger asked for is not available.		
4 This dialogue takes place at the currency exchange counter.		

Wrap-Up

A Complete the sentences with the words or expressions you used in this unit.

carry-on bag	carry	emergency	proceed	aisle
security bin	take off	throw away	turn right	upstairs

1 Would you like a window or _____ seat?

2 Do you have a seat by the _____ exit?

3 Please put your _____ through the X-ray machine.

4 Do I have to _____ my jacket?

5 Please put your laptop computer in the _____.

6 Can I _____ this bottled water?

7 Please _____ through the metal detector.

8 I'll have to _____ this water first.

9 It's _____ on the third floor.

10 Just take the escalator on your left and then _____.

B Put the following steps for passing through the automated immigration machine in the correct order.

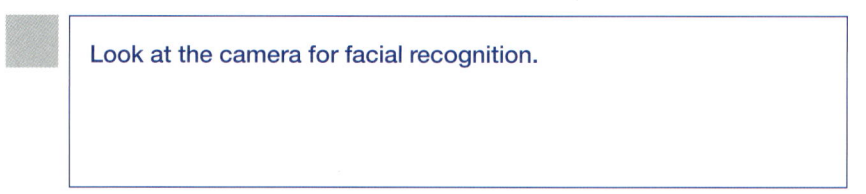 Look at the camera for facial recognition.

 Proceed through the entry doors when they open.

 Scan your passport.

 Put your registered finger on the scanner.

Unit 04 Welcome Aboard!

In this unit, you will learn:
1. How to get information from the flight information board
2. How to guide passengers on board
3. The items onboard commercial airplanes

Warm-Up

Look at the flight departure board. Then, ask and answer the questions with your partner.

✈ DEPARTURE

Flight	Destination	Departure Time	Gate	Status
CX417	Hong Kong	5:20	42	Gate Closed
KE305	London	8:20	41	Gate Closed
LH715	Frankfurt	9:45	36	Boarding
SQ6935	Chicago	10:10	28	Boarding
NH568	Yokohama	14:30	15	Delayed
CA246	Tianjin	16:35	19	Canceled
OZ752	Bangkok	18:40	14	On Time

A What time does Flight _____ depart?

B It departs at _____.

A What's the gate number for Flight _____?

B It's _____.

A Where does Flight _____ go?

B It goes to _____.

A What's the status of Flight _____?

B It's / The gate is _____.

Vocabulary

Complete the following sentences by using the words from the box.

| aboard | belongings | devices | fasten | help ~ with |
| lavatory | overhead bin | run out of | take off | upright |

1 Put your carry-on item above you in the _____.

2 Please turn off all electronic _____ until the seatbelt sign goes off.

3 Would you please return your seat to the _____ position?

4 Can I _____ you _____ those bags?

5 I'm sorry, but we've _____ that item.

6 You can use the _____ after takeoff.

7 I feel quite nervous whenever planes _____.

8 Please take your seats and _____ your seatbelts.

9 The plane is about to leave. You'd better get _____ now.

10 Don't forget to take all of your personal _____ with you.

Listen Up

Listen to the boarding announcement and choose T (true) or F (false). 04-01

		T	F
1	Passengers will begin boarding in 15 minutes.	☐	☐
2	First-class passengers must board first.	☐	☐
3	SkyTeam Elite members are asked to board second.	☐	☐
4	Passengers with babies can board at any time.	☐	☐
5	Economy-class passengers from row 46 and lower should board last.	☐	☐

Let's Talk ❶ Listen to the conversation and practice it with your partner. 04-02

Boarding

Cabin Crew Member	Good morning. Welcome aboard. May I see your boarding pass, please?
Passenger	Yes, here you are.
Cabin Crew Member	Thank you. Please take the aisle to the right. May I help you with your belongings?
Passenger	Yes, please. They're a bit heavy.
Cabin Crew Member	Would you please put your bag under the seat in front of you?
Passenger	Can I put it in the overhead bin?
Cabin Crew Member	Oh, sure. Let me help you with it.
Passenger	Thank you so much!

Role-Play

Practice the conversation with your partner again. Use the ideas in the box.

A Good morning. Welcome aboard. May I see your boarding pass, please?

B Yes, here you are.

A Thank you. Please ❶_____. May I help you with your ❷_____?

B Yes, please. It's a bit heavy.

A Would you please put your bag ❸_____?

B Can I put it in the overhead bin?

A Oh, sure. Let me help you with it.

B Thank you so much!

❶ Directions to Give	❷ Carry-On Item	❸ Place to Keep the Item
take the aisle to the left	package	under your seat
go straight to the middle of the cabin	box	in the back of the cabin
go upstairs	coat	in the closet
go to the front	laptop	under the seat in front of you

Language Practice

A Look at the pictures. Then, complete the polite requests by using the phrases in the box.

put your bag in the overhead bin	shut the window shade
turn off your cell phone	fasten your seatbelt
return your seat to the upright position	remain seated

1 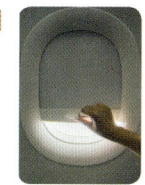   2 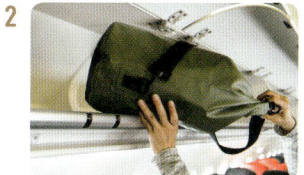   3

4    5    6

1 Would you please _____?   4 Would you please _____?

2 Would you please _____?   5 Would you please _____?

3 Would you please _____?   6 Would you please _____?

B Look at the following in-flight announcement and choose T (true) or F (false).

> Ladies and gentlemen, the captain has turned on the fasten seatbelt sign. Please put your carry-on luggage underneath the seat in front of you or in an overhead bin. Please sit down and fasten your seatbelts. And make sure your seatbacks and folding trays are in their full, upright positions. If you are sitting next to an emergency exit, please read the instruction card located by your seat. If you do not wish to assist in an emergency, please ask a flight attendant to reseat you. At this time, please turn off all electronic devices until we fly to above 10,000 feet. We will notify you when you may use these devices. This is a nonsmoking flight. You may not smoke anywhere on the airplane, including in the lavatories. Thank you.

		T	F
1	Passengers must fasten their seatbelts.	☐	☐
2	Passengers may keep their carry-on bags in their seats.	☐	☐
3	Passengers may not recline their seats at this time.	☐	☐
4	Passengers can use any electronic devices.	☐	☐
5	Under no circumstances is smoking allowed on this flight.	☐	☐

Let's Talk ❷ Listen to the conversation and practice it with your partner. 🔊 04-03

Reading Material Service

Cabin Crew Member	Excuse me. Would you please fasten your seatbelt?
Passenger	Yes, of course. Could you give me another blanket and a pillow?
Cabin Crew Member	All right, sir. Please wait a moment while I get them.
Passenger	One more thing, please. Do you have any newspapers or magazines on the plane?
Cabin Crew Member	We have some fashion, business, and current events magazines and several newspapers.
Passenger	Can I have a *Sports Daily*?
Cabin Crew Member	I'm sorry, sir. We've run out of it. Would you like a *Sports Herald* instead?
Passenger	Yes, that would be great.

Role-Play

Practice the conversation with your partner again. Use the ideas in the box.

A Excuse me. Would you please fasten your seatbelt?

B Yes, of course. Could you give me another blanket and a pillow?

A All right, sir. Please wait a moment while I get them.

B One more thing, please. Do you have any newspapers or magazines on the plane?

A We have some fashion, business, and current events magazines and several newspapers.

B Can I have a(n) ❶_____?

A I'm sorry, sir. ❷_____. Would you like a(n) ❸_____ instead?

B Yes, that would be great.

❶ Newspaper / Magazine Requested	❷ Current Condition	❸ Alternative
New York Times	We're all out	Washington Post
Korea Times	We don't have any copies left	Korea Herald
Vogue	It was not loaded	Elle Paris
Economist	We don't carry that magazine on this flight	Business Weekly

Language Practice

A Look at the in-flight safety announcement and choose T (true) or F (false).

> Ladies and gentlemen, on behalf of the crew, I ask you to direct your attention to the monitors while we review the emergency procedures. This aircraft has six emergency exits. Take a minute to locate the exit closest to you. Please be aware that it may be behind you. Count the number of rows to that exit. Should the cabin experience sudden pressure loss, remain calm and listen for instructions from the cabin crew. Oxygen masks will drop from above your seat. Place the mask over your mouth and nose like this. Then, pull the strap to tighten it. If you are traveling with children, put your own mask on first before you help your children. In the unlikely event of an emergency landing and evacuation, leave all of your carry-on items behind. Life vests are located below your seats, and emergency lighting will lead you to the closest exit and slide. Please make sure that all of your carry-on luggage is stowed safely during the flight. As we wait for takeoff, please review the safety data card which is located in the seat pocket in front of you.

		T	F
1	There are ten emergency exits on this aircraft.	☐	☐
2	If passengers are traveling with children, they should help the children put on their oxygen masks first.	☐	☐
3	In an emergency, passengers should leave all their carry-on items behind.	☐	☐
4	Life vests are located in the seat pockets in front of passengers.	☐	☐

B Match each question with the appropriate response.

1. Would you please fold your tray table? _____
2. Would you like a newspaper or magazine? _____
3. Can you help me put my luggage in that compartment above? _____
4. Fasten your seatbelt, please. _____
5. Would you bring your seatback to the full, upright position? _____

> a. Oh, I'm sorry. I thought it was up.
> b. Let me put it in the next one. It has more room.
> c. Can I get a magazine?
> d. But I don't like to wear it. It's uncomfortable.
> e. Yes, of course. But I don't know how to close it.

Practice More

A Listen to the dialogue. Then, complete the following script. 04-04

Seatbelts

Cabin Crew Member	Excuse me. Would you please ¹_____ your seatbelt?
Passenger	I'm sorry. I don't know how to do that.
Cabin Crew Member	Oh, just ²_____ it this way.
Passenger	Is this all right?
Cabin Crew Member	Sure. One more thing. Would you ³_____ returning your seat to its upright position, please?
Passenger	Okay.

B Listen to the dialogue. Then, answer the following questions. 04-05

Separated Passengers

1. What does the passenger ask for?
2. Will the passenger change seats?
3. Where are the empty seats located?

C Listen to the dialogue. Then, put the following sentences in the correct order. 04-06

Changing Seats

1. I'm sorry, but I'm afraid there are no empty seats in the front. How about a seat in the middle of the cabin?
2. No, thank you.
3. In the front if possible.
4. Where would you like to sit, sir?
5. Excuse me, stewardess. May I change seats?

D Listen to the dialogue. Then, choose T (true) or F (false). 04-07

Lavatory Information	T	F
1 The passenger does not know where the lavatory is.		
2 Passengers are not allowed to use the lavatory during takeoff.		
3 The passenger cannot use the lavatory.		

Wrap-Up

A Complete the sentences with the words or expressions you used in this unit.

| fasten | have | instead | put | boarding pass |
| takeoff | to the right | together | with | upright position |

1. Would you please _____ your seatbelt?
2. Would you mind using it after _____?
3. Do you have any empty seats _____?
4. Would you like a *Sports Herald* _____?
5. Please take the aisle _____.
6. Would you please return your seat to its _____?
7. May I see your _____, please?
8. May I help you _____ your belongings?
9. Would you please _____ your bag under the seat in front of you?
10. Can I _____ a *Sports Daily*?

B Match each question with the appropriate response.

1. I want to read a book, but it's a little dark here. _____
2. Excuse me. I feel cold. _____
3. My headphones are not working. _____
4. I have a sore throat. _____
5. Can I use the lavatory now? _____

a. Oh, I'm sorry. I'll bring you another one.
b. I'll give you some medicine.
c. Here's the reading light button.
d. I'll bring an extra blanket.
e. I'm sorry. But would you mind using it after takeoff?

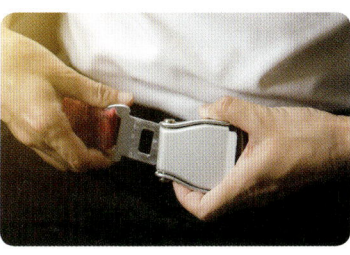  

Unit 05
Would You Like Something to Drink?

In this unit, you will learn:
1. How to request in-flight meals
2. How to buy duty-free items
3. How to fill out entry cards

Warm-Up

A Look at the special in-flight meals. Then, complete the special meal requests below and ask and answer the questions with your partner.

Types of Special Meals	Special Features
Infant Meal	It is a meal for infants 2 years old or younger.
Children's Meal	It is a meal for children between the ages of 3 and 12.
Vegetarian Meal	It is for people who do not eat meat.
Hindu Meal	It does not contain any beef.
Muslim Meal	It is prepared according to Halal rules, and there is no pork or alcohol.
Kosher Meal	It is prepared according to Jewish dietary rules.
Diabetic Meal	It does not contain any sugar.

Flight Attendant What would you like to have?

Passenger 1 I am with my 2-year-old baby. I would like to have an _____.

Passenger 2 I don't eat meat at all. I want to request a _____.

Passenger 3 I'm Jewish, and I keep kosher. I want to have a _____.

B Look at the list of in-flight services commercial airlines provide. What other services will you need during a flight? Discuss the topic with your partner.

in-flight meals	headsets
in-flight duty-free sales	newspapers/magazines
snacks and beverages	movies
music on demand	video on demand

Vocabulary

Complete the following sentences by using the words from the box.

| accept | airsickness | cabin crew | carry | change |
| delicious | medicine | on the rocks | operates | vegetarians |

1. Our airline _____ flights to 25 countries.
2. The _____ provides services for all the passengers on the flight.
3. How would you like your whiskey, straight or _____?
4. I'm afraid we don't _____ papaya juice on this flight.
5. The restaurant provides a special meal for _____.
6. I'm sorry, but we only _____ cash and plastic.
7. I have a sore throat. Please give me some _____.
8. The passenger suffered from _____ and felt bad for the entire flight.
9. Excuse me. I think you gave me the wrong _____. You gave me $15 instead of $25.
10. The apple pie you made was very _____.

Listen Up

Listen to the dialogue and choose T (true) or F (false).

	T	F
1 The flight is a joint service operated by Koreana Air and Dell Airlines.	☐	☐
2 The flight time to New York will be 14 hours and 30 minutes.	☐	☐
3 The flight departed on time.	☐	☐
4 Computers can be used when the seatbelt sign goes off.	☐	☐
5 The passengers may not use radios at any time.	☐	☐

Let's Talk ❶   Listen to the conversation and practice it with your partner. 05-02

Meal Service

Cabin Crew Member	Would you like something to drink? We have soda, juice, wine, and whiskey.
Passenger	Can I have some apple juice, please?
Cabin Crew Member	Here you are, sir. We have beef, fish, and *bibimbap* for dinner. What would you like to have?
Passenger	How is the fish cooked?
Cabin Crew Member	The fish is steamed in soy sauce. It is served with vegetables.
Passenger	I'll have the beef with some red wine, please.
Cabin Crew Member	Certainly, sir. Here you are and enjoy your meal!
Passenger	Thanks a lot.

Role-Play

Practice the conversation with your partner again. Use the ideas in the box.

A Would you like something to drink? We have soda, juice, wine, and whiskey.

B Can I have some ❶_____, please?

A Here you are, sir. We have ❷_____. for dinner. What would you like to have?

B How is the fish cooked?

A The fish is steamed in soy sauce. It is served with vegetables.

B I'll have the ❸_____ with some ❹_____, please.

A Certainly, sir. Here you are and enjoy your meal!

B Thanks a lot.

❶ Beverage	❷ Choice of Meal	❸ Your Choice	❹ Additional Request
cola	fish / pork / shrimp	pork	mineral water
grapefruit juice	ssambap / noodles / fish	noodles	whiskey
Scotch whiskey	beef / fish / *galbi jjim*	fish	white wine
beer	fish / chicken / beef	chicken	pretzels & nuts

Language Practice

A Look at the dialogue patterns in the box. Make your own dialogue with your partner by using the words below.

Passenger	Let me have some guava juice, please.
Cabin Crew Member	I'm sorry, but I'm afraid we don't carry it on this flight. Would you care for something else?
Passenger	Can I have some beer?
Cabin Crew Member	We have Korean beer, Japanese beer, and European beer. Which one would you like?
Passenger	I'll have European beer, please.

1. Dr. Pepper / wine (red wine / white wine)

2. root beer / tea (Lipton tea / Japanese tea)

3. milk tea / whiskey (American whiskey / Scotch whiskey)

B Match each question with the appropriate response.

1. Could I have another beer? _____

2. Do you have any pineapple juice? _____

3. Can I have some coffee? _____

4. I don't feel like eating right now. Can I have my meal later? _____

5. I'd like to have the beef. _____

6. I don't think this meal is hot enough. _____

a. I am sorry. We don't have pineapple juice, but we have orange juice and apple juice.
b. I am sorry. We just ran out of beef. How about chicken?
c. I am sorry, sir. I'll warm it up for you.
d. Sure. Any milk or sugar?
e. I am sorry, sir. You have already had two cans of beer.
f. Sure. Please let me know when you feel hungry.

Let's Talk 2

Listen to the conversation and practice it with your partner.

In-Flight Duty-Free Sales

Cabin Crew Member	Would you like to buy any duty-free items?
Passenger	Yes, I want to buy a bottle of Chanel No. 5.
Cabin Crew Member	Certainly, sir. That'll be 142 dollars.
Passenger	Do you take Thai baht?
Cabin Crew Member	I'm sorry, but we don't. We only accept U.S. dollars, euros, and Korean won.
Passenger	Oh, I have some euros. How much is it in euros?
Cabin Crew Member	It's 121 euros and 30 cents.
Passenger	Here you are.
Cabin Crew Member	Thank you, sir. Here is your change.

Role-Play

Practice the conversation with your partner again. Use the ideas in the box.

A Would you like to buy any duty-free items?

B Yes, I want to buy ❶_____.

A Certainly, sir. That'll be ❷_____ dollars.

B Do you take Thai baht?

A I'm sorry, but we don't. We only accept ❸_____ dollars.

B Oh, I have some euros. How much is it in euros?

A It's ❹_____.

B Here you are.

A Thank you, sir. Here is your change.

❶ Shopping Item	❷ Price in U.S. Dollars	❸ Acceptable Currencies	❹ Price in Euros
a crystal necklace	225	U.S. dollars, euros	162.35
sunglasses	175	U.S. dollars, euros, British pounds	126.25
a men's wallet	195	U.S. dollars, euros, Japanese yen	140.70
a malt whiskey	90	U.S. dollars, euros, Korean won	64.95

Language Practice

A Complete the table about some currencies and the countries that use them. Then, check your answer with your partner.

Country	Currency
Korea	
	pound
Philippines	
China	
European Union	
	yen
	baht

B Look at the currency exchange rate table and practice the dialogue by using the rates.

Currency	Korean Won
U.S. Dollar	1,140
British Pound	1,490
Euro	1,330
Australian Dollar	900
Canadian Dollar	910
Japanese Yen	1,020
Chinese Yuan	170
Thai Baht	35

A   What is the exchange rate for _____ to Korean won?

B   _____ is worth 1,140 Korean won.

A   Okay. I'd like to change 300,000 Korean won into _____ , please. How much will I get?

B   You will get _____ . Here you are.

A   Thank you very much.

Practice More

A Listen to the dialogue. Then, complete the following script. 🔊 05-04

Coffee Service

Cabin Crew Member	¹_____ you like some coffee, sir?
Passenger	Yes, please.
Cabin Crew Member	²_____ your cup on the tray, please. Thank you, sir. Do you need any ³_____ or sugar?
Passenger	Cream only.
Cabin Crew Member	It's ⁴_____ hot. Please be careful.

B Listen to the dialogue. Then, answer the following questions. 🔊 05-05

Meal Service

1. What does the cabin crew member want to know?
2. What will the cabin crew member take away?
3. Did the passenger enjoy his meal?

C Listen to the dialogue. Then, put the following sentences in the correct order. 🔊 05-06

Passenger Requests

1. Can you tell me what *bibimbap* is?
2. Here's the *bibimbap*. You can add the sesame oil and *gochujang* that are on the tray. *Gochujang* is a Korean red chili paste. It can be spicy, so just add a little at a time.
3. Okay, I'll try that.
4. Thank you. It looks delicious!
5. Sure. It's a Korean rice dish served with seasoned vegetables, ground beef, and a sauce.

D Listen to the dialogue. Then, choose T (true) or F (false). 🔊 05-07

Handling a Sick Passenger	T	F
1 The passenger has a stomachache.		
2 The passenger may feel nauseous.		
3 The cabin crew member will bring some medicine.		

Wrap-Up

A Complete the sentences with the words or expressions you used in this unit.

| accept | carry | duty-free | enjoy | finished |
| let | Muslim meal | place | something | would that be |

1. Would you like _____ to drink?
2. _____ me have some apple juice, please.
3. I'm sorry, but I'm afraid we don't _____ it on this flight.
4. Here you are and _____ your meal!
5. I am a Muslim. I would like to have a _____.
6. Would you like to buy any _____ items, sir?
7. How much _____ in euros?
8. We only _____ U.S. dollars, euros, and Korean won.
9. Have you _____ your meal?
10. _____ your cup on the tray, please.

B Fill out the entry card form.

1. Family name _____
2. First name(s) _____
3. Sex ☐ M ☐ F   4. Date of birth _____
5. Town and country of birth _____
6. Nationality _____
7. Occupation _____
8. Contact address (in full) _____
9. Passport no. _____
10. Place of issue _____
11. Length of stay _____
12. Port of last departure _____
13. Arrival flight/train number/ship name
_____
14. Signature _____

Unit 06: What's the Purpose of Your Visit?

In this unit, you will learn:
1 How to communicate at immigration and customs
2 How to use the quantifiers *much* and *many*
3 About facilities in international airports

Warm-Up

A What's the purpose of each passenger's visit? Match each sentence with the correct picture.

1 I'm on vacation.
2 I'm here on a business trip.
3 I'm on a group tour to go sightseeing.
4 I'm visiting my aunt in Brooklyn.
5 I'm going to attend a conference.

 a.
 b.
 c.
 d.
 e.

B Match the descriptions with the correct places at the airport.

1 The place where passengers get their baggage after a flight
2 A facility where passengers can exchange one currency for another
3 The place where officials check the passports of everyone entering the country
4 The place where your bags are checked for illegal goods when you enter a country
5 The place where lost items are kept until someone claims them

a. Customs
b. Currency Exchange
c. Baggage Claim
d. Immigration
e. Lost and Found

Vocabulary

Complete the following sentences by using the words from the box.

| carousel | connect | customs | declare | deplane |
| homestay | inspection | occupations | purpose | restricted |

1 From Chicago, you can _____ to all other American Airlines destinations.

2 The _____ of visiting America is to attend the Air Transport Research Society World Conference.

3 Try a _____ in Japan and live with a Japanese family during your trip.

4 The speed is _____ to 30 kilometers an hour here.

5 If you are carrying more than $10,000, you must _____ it to a customs officer.

6 After your plane lands, get your passport stamped at immigration and then get your bags checked at _____.

7 At baggage claim, the suitcases go around on the _____ until people pick them up.

8 Officials came to carry out a safety _____.

9 Many of today's good _____, including medical doctors and professors, will disappear in the next 30 years.

10 Please be considerate of other passengers when you _____.

Listen Up

Listen to the in-flight announcement and choose T (true) or F (false). 06-01

		T	F
1	The plane landed 10 minutes ago.	☐	☐
2	Passengers can place their laptop computers in their seats now.	☐	☐
3	Flight 21 is going to Chicago.	☐	☐
4	The flight to Dallas leaves from Gate 11.	☐	☐
5	There is a connecting flight to Detroit.	☐	☐

Let's Talk ❶

Listen to the conversation and practice it with your partner.

Immigration

Official   Good morning. May I see your passport, please?

Passenger   Here you are.

Official   What's the purpose of your visit?

Passenger   I'm here to study English.

Official   I see. How long are you going to stay in the United States?

Passenger   I'm planning to stay here for about 10 months.

Official   Okay. Where will you be staying?

Passenger   I will be staying with a host family. I'm doing a homestay.

Role-Play

Practice the conversation with your partner again. Use the ideas in the box.

A   Good morning. May I see your passport, please?

B   Here you are.

A   What's the purpose of your visit?

B   ❶_____.

A   I see. How long are you going to stay in the United States?

B   I'm planning to stay here for ❷_____.

A   Okay. Where will you be staying?

B   I will be ❸_____.

❶ Visiting Purpose	❷ Period of Stay	❸ Place of Stay
Business	a couple of weeks	staying at the Marriott Hotel on Lexington Avenue
Vacation	a week	staying at the Crowne Plaza Resort
I'm visiting my family	about a month	staying at my sister's house in Manhattan
I'm attending a conference	five days	staying in a residence hall at the university

Language Practice

A Look at some examples of impolite expressions. Then, change the expressions into polite ones.

Don't smoke here!	→	I'm sorry, but this is a nonsmoking area.
What's your passport number?	→	May I have your passport number, please?
		Would you let me know your passport number?
Put your bag in the overhead bin.	→	Would you put your bag in the overhead bin?
		Put your bag in the overhead bin, please.

1 Don't take photos here. →

2 What's your final destination? →

3 Wait behind the yellow line. →

4 What's your occupation? →

5 Turn off the electronic devices. →

B Read the following in-flight announcement and choose T (true) or F (false). Then, practice the announcement.

> Ladies and gentlemen, welcome to John F. Kennedy International Airport. The local time is 9:05 PM on June 12, and the temperature is 80 degrees Fahrenheit, or 27 degrees Celsius. For your safety and comfort, please remain seated with your seatbelts fastened until the captain turns off the seatbelt sign. Please be careful when opening the overhead bins as heavy articles may have shifted around during the flight. If you require deplaning assistance, please remain in your seat until all the other passengers have deplaned. On behalf of Koreana Airlines and the entire crew, I would like to thank you for joining us on this trip, and we look forward to seeing you on board again. Have a nice day!

		T	F
1	The plane has just landed at the airport.	☐	☐
2	Passengers can unfasten their seatbelts now.	☐	☐
3	If passengers require assistance deplaning, they should get off last.	☐	☐
4	Passengers should be careful when opening the overhead bins because articles may be easily mistaken for another passenger's articles.	☐	☐

Let's Talk ❷ Listen to the conversation and practice it with your partner. 06-03

Customs Inspection

Official   Do you have anything to declare?

Passenger   No, I have nothing to declare.

Official   Do you have any fruits, plants, vegetables, or meat?

Passenger   No, I don't. But I have some wine.

Official   How much wine do you have?

Passenger   I only have a bottle.

Official   That's okay. Do you have more than 10,000 U.S. dollars?

Passenger   No, I don't. I only have 300 U.S. dollars.

Official   No problem. Please proceed to the exit marked "Nothing to Declare."

Passenger   Thanks. I appreciate it.

Role-Play

Practice the conversation with your partner again. Use the ideas in the box.

A   Do you have anything to declare?

B   No, I have nothing to declare.

A   Do you have any fruits, plants, vegetables, or meat?

B   No, I don't. But I have some ❶_____.

A   How ❷_____ do you have?

B   I only have ❸_____.

A   That's okay. Do you have more than 10,000 U.S. dollars?

B   No, I don't. I only have 300 U.S. dollars.

A   No problem. Please proceed to the exit marked "Nothing to Declare."

B   Thanks. I appreciate it.

❶ Item	❷ Quantifier	❸ Amount
Korean red chili paste	much _____	ten small tubes
soju (Korean liquor)	much _____	three packs
instant rice	much _____	five packets
cigarettes	many _____	two cartons

Language Practice

A Look at the examples of quantifiers. Then, complete the dialogues.

> Use **many** for countable nouns.
> **Q** How **many** sandwiches should I buy for the picnic?
> **A** You should buy at least 13 sandwiches.
>
> Use **much** for uncountable nouns.
> **Q** How **much** sugar do you want?
> **A** 2 teaspoons, please.

1. **Q** _____ cookies did she eat?
   A She ate a dozen cookies.

2. **Q** _____ fragrances did you buy for your girlfriend?
   A I bought three different fragrances of flowers.

3. **Q** _____ fur coats do you have?
   A None. I don't wear fur coats.

4. **Q** _____ coffee do you drink a day?
   A I usually drink three cups of coffee every day.

5. **Q** _____ wine can I bring into EU countries?
   A You can bring 2 liters of wine without paying taxes or duties.

6. **Q** _____ songs have you saved on your smartphone?
   A I really like to listen to songs day and night, so I have saved more than 350 songs.

B Look at the list of prohibited items in the box. Then, work in groups to give the reasons why they are banned.

more than $10,000	endangered animal furs or skins	live animals
ivory products	meat and milk products	insects
fruits	certain plants, bulbs, and seeds	weapons

1. **Plants**: You can't bring plants because they may damage farmers' crops.
2. **Weapons**: You can't bring weapons on a plane because people can use them to harm others.
3. **Insects**: Insects are banned because they might carry diseases.

Practice More

A Listen to the dialogue. Then, complete the following script. 06-04

Immigration Inspection

Official	Passport and ¹_____, please.
Passenger	Here you are.
Official	Place your ²_____ on the scanner, please.
Passenger	Here?
Official	Yes. Thank you. And ³_____ the camera, please.
Passenger	This one?
Official	Yes. ⁴_____ on a moment, please.
Passenger	Is it ⁵_____?
Official	Yes, that's good. Thank you.

B Listen to the dialogue. Then, answer the following questions. 06-05

Transit Passenger Information

1. Where is the passenger going?
2. Did the passenger make her connecting flight on time?
3. What time does Delta Airlines Flight 723 leave?

C Listen to the dialogue. Then, put the following sentences in the correct order. 06-06

Terminal Information

1. How can I get to Terminal 2?
2. Take the shuttle bus on the second floor and get off at the first stop. The Delta counter is on the third floor.
3. Where is the Delta counter?
4. It's in Terminal 2.
5. Thank you very much.

D Listen to the dialogue. Then, choose T (true) or F (false). 06-07

Customs Inspection

	T	F
1 The passenger has nothing to declare.		
2 The officer inspected the passenger's bag.		
3 There is money in the bag.		

Wrap-Up

A Complete the sentences with the words or expressions you used in this unit.

declare	exit	get to	hold	index finger
long	much	purpose	arrival	nothing

1 May I see your passport and _____ form?

2 What's the _____ of your visit?

3 How _____ are you going to stay in the United States?

4 Place your _____ on the scanner, please.

5 Look into the camera and _____ on a moment, please.

6 Do you have anything to _____?

7 I have _____ to declare.

8 How _____ wine do you have?

9 Please proceed to the _____ marked "Nothing to Declare."

10 How can I _____ Terminal 2?

B Compare low-cost airlines with traditional major airlines by using the information below.

	Low-Cost Carriers (LCC)	*Traditional Airlines Full-Service Carriers (FSC)*
Fare	Low	High
Booking through a Travel Agent	Partially available Sell tickets over the Internet	Available
Use of International or Hub Airports	Generally go to secondary airports	Yes
Use of E-Tickets or Ticketless Travel	Prefer e-tickets or ticketless travel	Sell limited number of e-tickets
Classes of Seats	Single class of seats	More than 3 classes of seats
In-Flight Services	Very limited Separate charges for in-flight services	Free in-flight services
Names of Airlines	Air Busan, Jin Air, Eastar Jet, T'way Air, Jeju Air, Air Seoul, Air Asia, Virgin Express, Ryanair, EasyJet, Southwest Airlines, ATA Airlines	Asiana Airlines, Korean Air, Singapore Airlines, American Airlines, Air France, Japan Airlines, KLM, Lufthansa, British Airways, Qantas

Unit 07 My Baggage Is Missing

In this unit, you will learn:
1 How to claim and find your lost baggage
2 How to fill out a property irregularity report form
3 How to describe the shapes and colors of your property

Warm-Up

A Look at the places found at the airport.

1
Information Desk

2
Elevator

3
Baggage Claim

4
Lost and Found

5
Bus Stop

6
Customs

7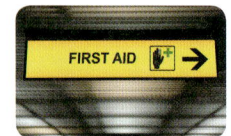
Medical Service

8
Tax Refund Counter

9
Internet Cafe

10
Car Rental Service

11
Subway Station

12
Currency Exchange

B Read the following questions and complete the answers.

1 Where do I go to collect my baggage? — You should go to _____.
2 Where do I go to use my computer? — You should go to _____.
3 Where do I go to get back the tax I paid while shopping at a store? — You should go to _____.
4 Where do I go to rent a car? — You should go to _____.
5 Where do I go to declare something? — You should go to _____.
6 Where do I go to report and find my lost belongings? — You should go to _____.
7 Where do I go to take a bus? — You should go to _____.
8 Where do I go to ask where the gift shop is? — You should go to _____.

Vocabulary

Complete the following sentences by using the words from the box.

| property | deliver | official | upset | conference |
| describe | fill out | inconvenience | irregularity | trace |

1 The Air Transport Research Society World _____ was held in Belgium for four days.

2 Many people tend to eat junk food when they are stressed or _____.

3 It's difficult to _____ his appearance.

4 Do I need to pick it up, or will they _____ it?

5 Please _____ the registration form and sign here.

6 The police are still trying to _____ the missing couple.

7 There may be a slight _____ in the size and shape of the product.

8 Always ask first if you want to use my _____.

9 We apologize for the _____ that this delay caused.

10 The _____ had the passenger look into the camera.

Listen Up

Listen to the dialogue and choose T (true) or F (false). 07-01

		T	F
1	People have similar bags, so passengers need to identify their bags by the check-in tag number.	☐	☐
2	The passenger could not find her baggage.	☐	☐
3	The official had the woman fill out a property irregularity report.	☐	☐
4	The passenger has just deplaned from Koreana Airlines.	☐	☐
5	The lost and found office is next to Gate 1.	☐	☐

Let's Talk 1

Listen to the conversation and practice it with your partner.

Lost and Found

Passenger   Excuse me. I've just arrived from New York, but my baggage is missing.

Official   May I see your baggage claim tag and your boarding pass, please?

Passenger   Yes, here they are.

Official   Would you fill out this form while we trace your baggage?

Passenger   I'm really upset. What happened to my bag?

Official   I am sorry for the inconvenience. Your baggage will arrive on the next flight from New York.

Passenger   Should I collect my baggage here?

Official   No. We will deliver it to your address.

Role-Play

Practice the conversation with your partner again. Use the ideas in the box.

A   Excuse me. I've just arrived from ❶_____, but my ❷_____ is/are missing.

B   May I see your baggage claim tag(s) and your boarding pass, please?

A   Yes, here they are.

B   Would you fill out this form while we trace your baggage?

A   I'm really upset. What happened to my bag?

B   I am sorry for the inconvenience. Your baggage will arrive on ❸_____.

A   Should I collect my baggage here?

B   No. We will deliver it to your address.

❶ Place of Departure	❷ Delayed Baggage	❸ Next Flight Available
Munich	golf club bag	KE023 from Seoul
Santiago	three boxes	OZ571 from Tokyo
Cape Town	backpack	UA639 from Hong Kong
Amsterdam	baby stroller	AA847 from Paris
Oslo	skis	NW008 from Jakarta

Language Practice

A Look at the property irregularity report (PIR) form below. Work in pairs. Complete the PIR form by asking your partner for the information you need.

> **Possible Questions:**
> 1 May I have your name?
> 2 May I have your email address?
> 3 Can I have your baggage tag number?
> 4 May I have your address here?
> 5 May I have your contact number?
> 6 What's in your baggage?
> 7 What does it look like?
> 8 When did you buy it?
> 9 How much did you pay for it?

Property Irregularity Report

1 Passenger's Name
2 Email Address
3 File Reference/Baggage Tag Number
4 Address
5 Phone Number
6 Description of Contents

Articles	Brand/Label	Color	Date of Purchase	Original Cost

This is to certify the accuracy of the above statement.

Date	Writer's Name	Signature

B Read the following lost baggage regulations. Then, discuss how much you can receive for the lost baggage above with your partner.

> Koreana Air follows the Warsaw Convention and cooperates the most it can. Liability for loss, delay, or damage to checked baggage is U.S. $20 per kg and U.S. $400 per passenger for carry-on baggage. However, it pays more for baggage that has been declared and additional charges paid at check-in. Koreana Air will not pay for laptop computers, camcorders, cameras, valuable instruments, jewelry, cash, securities, negotiable papers (contracts), samples, medication, antiques, fragile articles, or other similar valuable items contained in checked or unchecked baggage. Passengers should carry these items.

Let's Talk ❷   Listen to the conversation and practice it with your partner.

Baggage Claim

Official	How many bags are you missing?
Passenger	Just one. I need it before 9 AM.
Official	Okay. Could you please describe it for me?
Passenger	Sure. It's a regular black suitcase with two wheels.
Official	What size is it?
Passenger	It's medium sized. When can I get my bag?
Official	We will contact you as soon as we find it.
Passenger	Please hurry. I need my suit for a conference meeting.

Role-Play

Practice the conversation with your partner again. Use the ideas in the box.

A	How many bags are you missing?
B	Just one. I need it before 9 AM.
A	Okay. Could you please describe it for me?
B	Sure. It's a ❶_____.
A	What size is it?
B	It's ❷_____. When can I get my bag?
A	We will contact you as soon as we find it.
B	Please hurry. I need ❸_____ for a conference meeting.

❶ Description	❷ Size	❸ Content
hard, rectangular suitcase	big sized	my articles
soft, square leather bag	small sized	the registration form
big canvas bag	around 3 feet long	my dress shoes
polka-dotted backpack	20x30 inches	those books

Language Practice

A Match each question with the appropriate response.

1 What color is your suitcase? _____

2 Is there anything in your bag? _____

3 What is your suitcase made of? _____

4 What size is your baggage? _____

5 What kind of bag is it? _____

> a. It is made of plastic.
> b. Mine is orange with a blue tag.
> c. Yes, there are some clothes and books.
> d. It is a striped black leather golf bag.
> e. It is a big-sized brown hard suitcase with four wheels.

B Read the dialogue at the lost and found office. Then, make your own dialogue with your partner.

> Traveler   Excuse me. I'd like to report some lost property.
> Official   What does it look like?
> Traveler   It's a slim, metallic silver digital camera.
> Official   Where did you last see it?
> Traveler   In the cafeteria on the second floor.

1 laptop computer / at the immigration counter

2 diary wallet / at the currency exchange counter

3 suitcase / in the baggage claim area

4 shopping bag / by the telephone booth

5 smartphone / in the drugstore

Practice More

A Listen to the dialogue. Then, complete the following script. 07-04

Baggage Claim Information

Passenger Excuse me. Could you please tell me where I can ¹_____ my bags?

Official Certainly. Which flight did you ²_____?

Passenger I came from Seoul, Korea. I don't know the flight number.

Official No problem. Were you ³_____ on Koreana Air?

Passenger That's right.

Official Then you can pick up your baggage at ⁴_____ number 11.

B Listen to the dialogue. Then, answer the following questions. 07-05

Delayed Baggage

1 What happened to the passenger's bag?

2 What does the passenger have to leave there?

3 What does the passenger need to sign?

C Listen to the dialogue. Then, put the following sentences in the correct order. 07-06

Lost Baggage

1. We apologize for any inconvenience this has caused you.
2. We haven't received any information from the airport you departed from. I recommend filling out a lost-and-found form.
3. Can you tell me what happened to my lost bags?
4. I don't understand why my bags didn't make it.

D Listen to the dialogue. Then, choose T (true) or F (false). 07-07

Baggage Complaints	T	F
1 The passenger is complaining about her delayed suitcase.		
2 The passenger's suitcase has been broken.		
3 The passenger has to describe the items in her suitcase.		

Wrap-Up

A Complete the sentences with the words or expressions you used in this unit.

| baggage claim tag | regular | as soon as | describe | inconvenience |
| PIR | deliver | collect | arrive | missing |

1 I've just arrived from New York, but my baggage is _____.
2 May I see your _____ and your boarding pass, please?
3 Would you fill out a _____ form?
4 Could you please _____ your suitcase for me?
5 It's a _____ black suitcase with two wheels.
6 Your baggage will _____ on the next flight.
7 I am sorry for the _____.
8 Should I _____ my baggage here?
9 We will _____ it to your address.
10 We will contact you _____ we find it.

B Read the following article about the rights of passengers. Then, discuss it with your group.

Liability
You may claim up to 1,131 Special Drawing Rights (SDR) for damages caused by the destruction, damage, loss, or delay of your baggage on a flight by an EU airline anywhere in the world. However, airlines shall not be liable if they have taken all reasonable measures to avoid the damages or if it was impossible to take such measures.

Long delays
You may request a refund of your ticket if the delay exceeds five hours but only if you decide not to travel.

Cancelation
Financial compensation is due unless you were informed 14 days before the flight, or you were rerouted close to your original times, or the airline can prove that the cancelation was caused by extraordinary circumstances.

Assistance by airlines
Depending on the circumstances, if you are denied boarding or your flight is canceled or delayed, you may be entitled to receive assistance (catering, communications, and an overnight stay if necessary). In the event of denied boarding or cancelation, you may be offered the option of continuing your trip or receiving a refund on your ticket.

Unit 08

I'd Like a Double Room with an Ocean View

In this unit, you will learn:
1 Types of accommodations and hotel rooms
2 How to reserve a hotel room
3 How to check in at a hotel

Warm-Up

A The following are kinds of accommodations. Match each definition with the correct accommodation.

a. B&B	b. boutique hotel	c. guesthouse	d. hostel	e. hotel
f. inn	g. lodge	h. motel	i. residential hotel	j. resort hotel

1 _____ A place offering inexpensive accommodations, usually featuring shared bedrooms and communal facilities; ideal for budget travelers and backpackers

2 _____ A small rural house used by people on vacation or occupied seasonally by enthusiasts in sports such as skiing and hunting

3 _____ An intimate, independently run lodging establishment, where breakfast is included in the room rate

B Which type of room will you choose in the following situations and why?

1 Three of you want to have an important meeting while staying overnight.
2 You will be staying overnight with your brother.
3 You will be taking a business trip alone.

single

twin

suite

double

double-double

Vocabulary

Complete the following sentences by using the words from the box.

| accommodations | charge | concierge | disappointing | peak |
| occupied | rate | receptionists | registration | suite |

1 Please fill out this _____ card. Your room is on the ninth floor.

2 A _____ is bigger and more luxurious than a typical standard hotel room.

3 A hotel _____ helps hotel guests with everything they need to have a pleasant stay.

4 Hotel _____ make guests feel welcome and deal with room bookings, cancelations, and other requests from guests.

5 I'm afraid all the rooms are already _____.

6 It's hard to make a reservation during the _____ season.

7 The restaurant's atmosphere was great, but the food was _____.

8 There's an extra _____ after midnight.

9 What is the _____ for the honeymoon suite?

10 Most universities in the USA provide _____ for first-year students.

Listen Up

Listen to the dialogue and choose T (true) or F (false). 08-01

		T	F
1	The guest wants to change his reservation.	☐	☐
2	The guest is going to stay for three nights.	☐	☐
3	The guest reserved a single room with a bath.	☐	☐
4	The guest's room is on the 15th floor.	☐	☐
5	The room rate is $125 per night.	☐	☐

Let's Talk ❶

Listen to the conversation and practice it with your partner. 🔊 08-02

Hotel Reservation

Receptionist	Good morning. Manhattan Hotel reservations. Lee speaking. How may I help you?
Guest	Hello. I'd like to book a room from June 4. Do you have any vacancies?
Receptionist	Yes, sir. We have several rooms available on that day. How long will you be staying?
Guest	I'll be staying for two nights.
Receptionist	How many people will be with you?
Guest	There will be two of us. I'd like a double room with an ocean view.
Receptionist	Great. May I have your name and contact number, please?
Guest	I'm Chuck Stockman, and my cell phone number is 773-246-4554.
Receptionist	All right, Mr. Stockman. Your reservation has been made for a double room with an ocean view for two nights from June 4.
Guest	Perfect. Thank you so much.

Role-Play

Practice the conversation with your partner again. Use the ideas in the box.

A Good morning. Manhattan Hotel reservations. Lee speaking. How may I help you?

B Hello. I'd like to book a room from ❶_____. Do you have any vacancies?

A Yes, sir. We have several rooms available on that day. How long will you be staying?

B I'll be staying for two nights.

A How many people will be with you?

B There will be ❷_____. I'd like ❸_____.

A Great. May I have your name and contact number, please?

B I'm ❹_____, and my cell phone number is 773-246-4554.

A All right, sir/ma'am. Your reservation has been made for ❶,❸_____.

B Perfect. Thank you so much.

❶ Date	❷ Number of People	❸ Type of Room	❹ Name
May 13	two	a twin room with a mountain view	(your name)
October 25	one	a single room on the highest floor	Tony Fessler
July 18	three	a suite with a downtown view	Patrick Liu

Language Practice

A Practice the dialogue with your partner by using the given length of stay. Try to use three different types of questions.

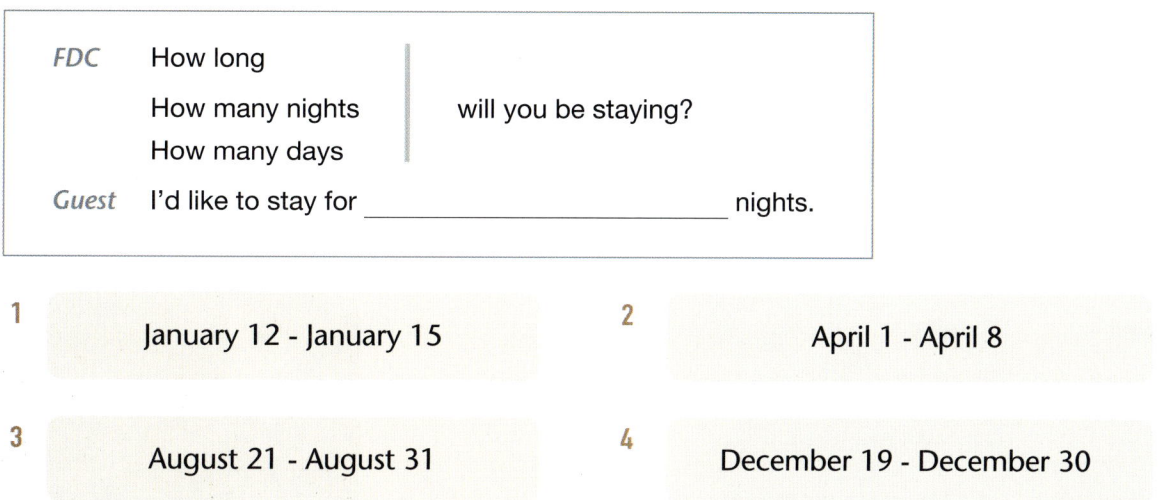

B Read the following confirmation email sent by the hotel and write your own email by using the same pattern.

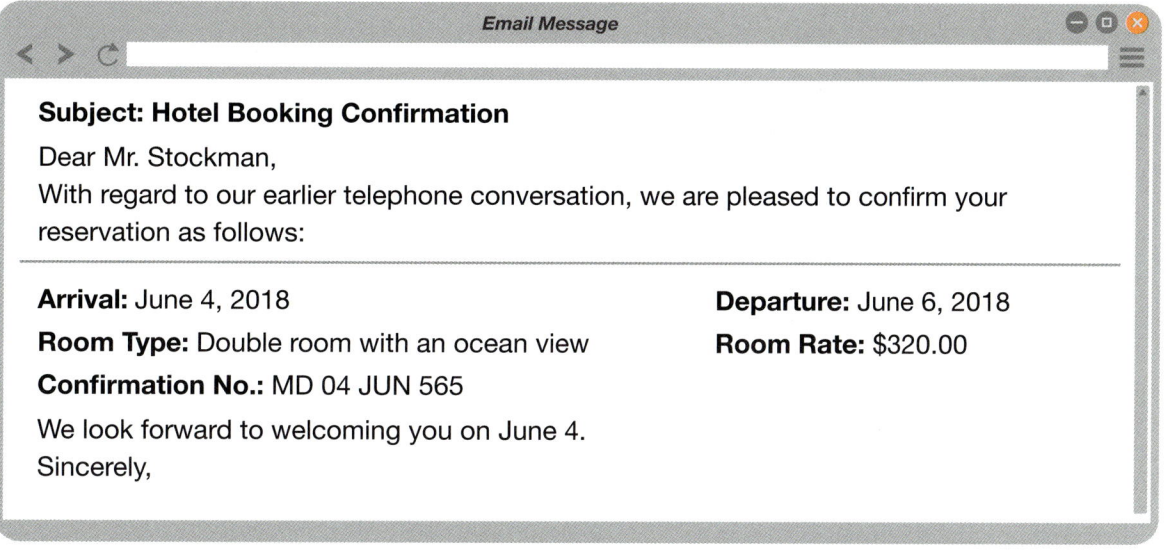

Let's Talk ❷   Listen to the conversation and practice it with your partner. 08-03

Hotel Check-In

Receptionist   Good afternoon, sir and madam. How may I help you?

Guest   I have a reservation. My name is Chuck Stockman.

Receptionist   Thank you, Mr. Stockman. Yes, you have a double room with an ocean view for two nights.

Guest   That's right. And I want my room to be located on a high floor.

Receptionist   Yes, your room is on the fifteenth floor. It's room 1505. Here is your key card.

Guest   Thank you.

Receptionist   Please fill out this registration card and sign here.

Guest   Sure. Where is the elevator?

Receptionist   The elevators are on your right next to the gift shop. Enjoy your stay.

Role-Play

Practice the conversation with your partner again. Use the ideas in the box.

A   Good afternoon, sir and madam. How may I help you?

B   I have a reservation. My name is Chuck Stockman.

A   Thank you, Mr. Stockman. Yes, you have a ❶_____ for two nights.

B   That's right. And I want my room to be located on a high floor.

A   Yes, your room is ❷_____. Here is your key card.

B   Thank you.

A   Please fill out this registration card and sign here.

B   Sure. Where is the elevator?

A   The elevators are ❸_____. Enjoy your stay.

❶ Type of Room	❷ Location of the Room	❸ Location of the Elevator
a twin room with an extra bed	on the 24th floor / room 2401	on your left beside the cafe
a suite with a river view	on the 8th floor / room 815	just around the corner
a king-sized bed with a downtown view	on the 18th floor / room 1806	across from the lobby

Language Practice

A Complete the following registration card by asking your partner. Then, compare the card with your group.

Hotel Registration Card

NAME:	**NATIONALITY:**
ADDRESS:	**CAR REGISTRATION NO.:**
DATE OF ARRIVAL:	**DATE OF DEPARTURE:**
METHOD OF PAYMENT:	☐ Credit Card ☐ Cash ☐ Check
ROOM RATE:	☐ DINNER, BED & BREAKFAST ☐ BED & BREAKFAST
NEWSPAPER ORDERED:	**CHECKOUT TIME:** 11 AM
SIGNATURE:	**ROOM NO.:**

Notes: Checks must be accompanied by a current bank card.
Credit cards must be imprinted and signed, amount to be verified prior to departure.
Cash customers can select to either pay in advance or on a day-to-day basis.

Possible questions:

1. Your name and nationality, please?
2. What's your address?
3. What's your car registration number?
4. Your arrival and departure date?
5. Are you going to use our dinner plan?
6. How would you like to pay?
7. Could you sign here, please?

B Match each question with the appropriate response.

1. Would you please fill out this registration card?
2. Could you show me your passport, please?
3. Would you like a smoking or nonsmoking room?
4. Could you please show me your ID?
5. Can I have your credit card for a moment?
6. Would you like a room on the top floor?

---

a. Either room would be fine.
b. Here's my driver's license.
c. No, I prefer one on a lower floor.
d. Should I fill in every blank?
e. Sure. Here's my Visa card.
f. Yes, I've got it right here.

Practice More

A Listen to the dialogue. Then, complete the following script. 08-04

No Rooms Available

FDC Good morning. Hyatt Reservation Desk. Susan speaking. Can I help you?

Guest Yes. Do you have a twin room ¹_____ for tomorrow night?

FDC Sorry. We are ²_____ for tomorrow night.

Guest How about a double room?

FDC I'm sorry, sir. It's the ³_____ season now.

Guest Oh, that's ⁴_____. Well, thank you anyway.

B Listen to the dialogue. Then, answer the following questions. 08-05

Changing Your Reservation

1 What is the room number originally assigned?

2 What does the guest ask for?

3 What floor will the guest stay on?

C Listen to the dialogue. Then, put the following sentences in the correct order. 08-06

Smoking or Nonsmoking?

1. No, thanks. I don't like smoking rooms.
2. How long will you be staying?
3. Do you have a room available for tonight? I have no reservation.
4. Good afternoon. May I help you?
5. Three nights.
6. Just a minute, ma'am. We only have smoking rooms left. Is that okay with you?

D Listen to the dialogue. Then, choose T (true) or F (false). 08-07

Different Room Rates	T	F
1 The woman wants a room with a mountain view.		
2 The additional charge is $30.00 per night.		
3 The total rate will be $210.00 per night.		

Wrap-Up

A Complete the sentences with the words or expressions you used in this unit.

| available | change | charge | extra bed | fill out |
| occupied | stay | take | view | would |

1. What kind of room _____ you like, ma'am?
2. There's an additional _____ for a room with an ocean view.
3. The guest said, "I will _____ it," as soon as he saw the room.
4. I'd like to _____ my reservation from May 5 to May 12.
5. I'd like to book it to a double room with an _____.
6. When would you like to _____, sir?
7. Do you have a twin room _____ for tomorrow night?
8. Your room is on the fifteenth floor and has an ocean _____.
9. Sorry. The rooms on the higher floors are all _____.
10. Would you _____ this form?

B Match the questions with the correct answers.

1. Can I have your registration card? — a. With a credit card.
2. Would you please fill out this form? — b. That's all right.
3. You'll be staying with us for two nights. — c. Sure. Can I borrow your pen?
4. How are you planning to pay? — d. I'm sorry, but we don't.
5. He will show you to your room. — e. Yes. Here you are.
6. Sorry to have kept you waiting. — f. That's great. Thank you.
7. Do you accept Korean currency? — g. Yes, that's correct.

Unit 09
We Have a Business Center on the Second Floor

In this unit, you will learn:
1. Various kinds of hotel services
2. How to request and complain about hotel services
3. How to check out

Warm-Up

Look at the various hotel services and facilities. Then, identify the services in the pictures.

Hotel Facilities	Hotel Services	Hotel Room Amenities
restaurant, lobby lounge, swimming pool, Internet, spa, sauna, massage, fitness center (gym), conference hall, meeting room, banquet hall, play room, bar, business center gift shop, tennis court, childcare center	**Room:** room service, housekeeping, heating and air conditioning, dry cleaning, laundry, Wi-Fi, international calls **Arrival and departure:** airport shuttle, express checkout, concierge, valet parking **Front desk:** wakeup call, currency exchange, information about events **Concierge:** baggage delivery, child care, wheelchair access, newspaper	TV, mini bar, coffee maker, safe, spa bath, telephone, iron and ironing board, complimentary bottled water, hair dryer, computer, towels and toiletries

Vocabulary

Complete the following sentences by using the words from the box.

| apologize | charge | clockwise | complimentary | declined |
| equipped | faucet | remove | request | safe |

1 I will _____ the wrong charge from your bill immediately.

2 Don't forget to turn off the _____ after using the washroom.

3 We offer _____ bottles of water to all of our guests.

4 Your TV is still under warranty, so we'll fix it free of _____.

5 I'll need a conference room _____ with a video system at 10:00 tomorrow morning.

6 Extra towels and pillows are available on _____.

7 Guests often keep their cameras, jewelry, and other valuables in their room _____.

8 I _____ for the mistake. I'll have it fixed as soon as possible.

9 Turn the key _____ to start the engine.

10 I'm sorry, but your credit card was _____. Do you have another one?

Listen Up

Listen to the dialogue and choose T (true) or F (false). 09-01

		T	F
1	A gift shop is on the third floor.	☐	☐
2	There is just one gift shop in the hotel.	☐	☐
3	The fitness center is on the 2nd floor.	☐	☐
4	The swimming pool is next to the restaurant.	☐	☐
5	The bar is in the basement.	☐	☐

Let's Talk ❶   Listen to the conversation and practice it with your partner. 09-02

Complaints and Requests

Receptionist Hello. Front Desk. How may I help you?

Guest Hi. This is room 902. I have a problem with the bathroom. There is no hot water.

Receptionist Oh, I'm very sorry, sir. I'll send someone up right away.

Guest And could you help me out with something else? Where is the business center?

Receptionist The business center is on the second floor.

Guest Thank you. One more thing. Could you please give me a wakeup call at 6:45 tomorrow morning?

Receptionist Certainly. A wakeup call at 6:45 for room 902.

Guest That's correct. Thank you.

Role-Play

Practice the conversation with your partner again. Use the ideas in the box.

A Hello. Front Desk. How may I help you?

B Hi. This is room 902. I have a problem with the ❶_____.

A Oh, I'm very sorry, sir. I'll send someone up right away.

B And could you help me out with something else? Where is the ❷_____?

A The ❷_____ is _____.

B Thank you. One more thing. Could you please give me a wakeup call at ❸_____ tomorrow morning?

A Certainly. A wakeup call at ❸_____ for room 902.

B That's correct. Thank you.

❶ Problem	❷ Facility and Location	❸ Time to Wake Up
air conditioner / It's not working	swimming pool / on the top floor	5:00
bathroom / There's no towel	bar / on the 2nd basement level	5:40
window / It's broken	gym / in the basement	6:15
Internet / The Wi-Fi isn't working	sauna / on the 3rd floor	6:30

Language Practice

A Write complaints by using the words below.

> I have a problem with the window. It won't open.

1. TV / turn on
2. safe / open
3. air conditioning / work
4. toilet / flush

B Look at the dialogues about complaints and requests. Then, make your own dialogues and practice them with your partner.

Complaint: No hot water

Receptionist   Hello. Front Desk. How may I help you?
Guest   This is room 515. I have a problem with the bathroom. There is no hot water coming from the faucet.
Receptionist   I'm sorry. I'll send someone up right away.
Guest   Thank you.

1. The room is too warm.
2. The fridge doesn't work.
3. The Wi-Fi in the room is too slow.
4. There's no TV remote control.

Request: Wakeup call

Receptionist   Hello. Front Desk. Can I help you?
Guest   This is room 806. Could you please give me a wakeup call at 6:30 tomorrow morning?
Receptionist   Sure. A wakeup call at 6:30 for room 806.
Guest   That's right. Thank you.

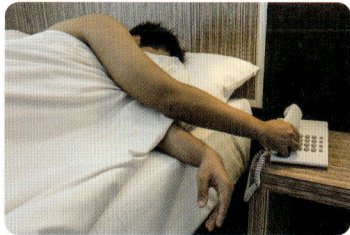

5. I need a wakeup call tomorrow.
6. What is the Wi-Fi password?
7. Can I get more toilet paper?
8. Is there a pool in this hotel?

Let's Talk ❷ Listen to the conversation and practice it with your partner.

Checking Out

Guest   Can I check out now? My name is Patrick Hill, and I'm in room 816. Here is the key card.

Receptionist   Thank you. Just a moment, please. I'll get your bill... Here you are, Mr. Hill. Your total is $525.75. That includes service charge and tax. Please check to see if everything is correct.

Guest   Let me see... I think it's all right.

Receptionist   How would you like to pay?

Guest   By credit card. Is that okay?

Receptionist   Certainly. Here is your receipt. I hope you enjoyed staying with us.

Guest   I had an excellent stay. Thank you.

Role-Play

Practice the conversation with your partner again. Use the ideas in the box.

A   Can I check out now? My name is ❶_____, and I'm in room ❶_____. Here is the key card.

B   Thank you. Just a moment, please. I'll get your bill... Here you are. Your total is ❷_____. That includes service charge and tax. Please check to see if everything is correct.

A   Let me see... I think it's all right.

B   How would you like to pay?

A   By ❸_____. Is that okay?

B   Certainly. Here is your receipt. I hope you enjoyed staying with us.

A   I had an excellent stay. Thank you.

❶ Guest's Name and Room Number	❷ Total Fees and Charges	❸ Payment Method
Susan Collins / 606	$312.25	credit card
Matthew Cobb / 567	$668.00	traveler's check
Giyeong Park / 2312	837,500 won	cash
Saori Riku / 327	1,030 yen	MasterCard

Language Practice

A Look at the following introductions of several hotel staff members. Then, explain what they do to your partner.

"I look after guests when they first arrive at a hotel. I check them in, take care of their complaints, and check them out."

→ A receptionist looks after guests when they first arrive at a hotel by checking them in, by taking care of their complaints, and by checking them out.

housekeeper

"I clean all the rooms for the hotel guests."

security guard

"I protect the hotel and make sure nothing bad happens here."

concierge

"I take care of our guests' needs and get them everything they want."

chef

"I cook food at a restaurant and prepare meals."

bellhop

"I carry guests' bags to their rooms."

B Discuss the following seven steps for handling guest complaints.

7 Steps for Handling Guest Complaints

1. **Listen and stay calm.**
   It's important to listen carefully to the guest and to see things from the guest's point of view.

2. **Acknowledge your guest's feelings and his/her right to complain.**
   Your guest paid a lot of money to stay at your hotel. He/She has the right to complain about an inconvenience.

3. **Figure out the problem and apologize.**
   Do not pretend to listen to your guest and then make an excuse. You should understand exactly what the problem is and apologize for the inconvenience.

4. **Suggest alternatives and agree on solution.**
   Just listening is not enough. You need to suggest a solution that your guest agrees to.

5. **Take action.**
   If your guest asks for more towels in his/her room, you should send them immediately.

6. **Record the incident.**
   Your record can prevent a recurrence of the incident.

7. **Follow up to ensure customer satisfaction.**
   After solving the problem, don't forget to ask your guest if the solution was satisfactory to him/her.

Practice More

A Listen to the dialogue. Then, complete the following script. 09-04

Guest Room Equipment

Bellhop   Here you are, Ms. Kim. This is your room.

Ms. Kim   Wow. It's very nice. But it's a little hot and humid in here.

Bellhop   We have air conditioning. Turn the switch clockwise to make the temperature cooler.

Ms. Kim   Where's the ¹_____?

Bellhop   It's right here. And this bottled water is ²_____.

Ms. Kim   Okay. Thank you very much.

B Listen to the dialogue. Then, answer the following questions. 09-05

Making Complaints about Hotel Rooms

1 What's the number of the room the guest is staying in?

2 What problem does the guest have?

3 What kind of TV program does the guest want to see?

C Listen to the dialogue. Then, put the following sentences in the correct order. 09-06

Asking to Keep Baggage

1. Could you keep my suitcases for a couple of hours?
2. Sure. How may I help you?
3. No problem. Take this tag with you. You need the tag when you reclaim them.
4. Room 2012. But I just checked out.
5. Excuse me. Can I ask you for a favor?
6. What is your room number?

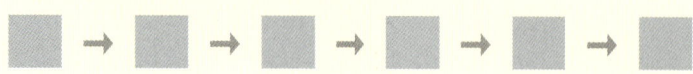

D Listen to the dialogue. Then, choose T (true) or F (false). 09-07

Correcting Mistakes

	T	F
1 The guest has a problem with the bill.		
2 The guest made an international call.		
3 The receptionist used the fax machine in the business center.		
4 This dialogue happens during checkout.		

Wrap-Up

A Complete the sentences with the words or expressions you used in this unit.

| give | mistake | keep | make | if |
| pay | problem with | reclaim | right away | turn |

1. I have a _____ the bathroom.
2. Please check to see _____ it is correct.
3. _____ the switch clockwise to make the temperature cooler.
4. I'll send someone up _____.
5. Could you please _____ me a wakeup call at 7:00 tomorrow morning?
6. How would you like to _____, sir?
7. There's a _____ on my bill.
8. Could you _____ my suitcases for a couple of hours?
9. Take this tag with you. You need the tag when you _____ them.
10. I didn't _____ any overseas calls from my room.

B Look at the opening and closing times of some hotel services. Ask and answer questions about the service hours with your partner.

Service	Opening Time	Closing Time
Breakfast Buffet	6:00 AM	10:00 AM
Coffee Shop	10:00 AM	11:00 AM
Swimming Pool	7:00 AM	10:00 AM
Fitness Club	7:00 AM	11:00 AM
Business Center	24 hours a day	24 hours a day
Room Service	24 hours a day	24 hours a day

A What time does the fitness club open?
B It opens at 7:00 AM.
A Can I use the business center early in the morning?
B Sure. It's open 24 hours a day.

Unit 10
What Kinds of Cars Do You Have?

In this unit, you will learn:
1. How to rent a car
2. How to ask for and give directions
3. The classes and types of cars
4. Road signs

Warm-Up

A Read about the types of cars. Select a car class from the list. Then, practice the dialogue with your partner.

> What class of car would you like to rent?

> I'd like to rent a full-size car. I think it's safe and comfortable.

Types of Cars

Economy car (subcompact car) · Very small and economical · Chevrolet Sonic, Hyundai Accent, Ford Fiesta, Kia Rio	**Compact car** · Small and economical · Chevrolet Cruze, Ford Focus, Kia Forte, Volkswagen Golf
Mid-size car · Intermediate and comfortable · Chevrolet Malibu, Ford Fusion, Hyundai Sonata, Honda Accord, Kia Optima, Nissan Altima, Toyota Camry	**Full-size car** · Large and comfortable · Chevrolet Impala, Ford Taurus, Toyota Avalon
Sports car · Performance and handling · Audi R8, Chevrolet Camaro, Dodge Challenger, Ford Mustang, Porsche 911	**Convertible** · Convert between open-air mode and enclosed mode · Bentley Continental GT Convertible, Chevrolet Camaro ZL1 Convertible
SUV (sport utility vehicle) · Four-wheel drive and off-road capability · Hyundai Santa Fe, Jeep Grand Cherokee, Nissan Murano, Chevrolet Equinox, Ford Edge	**Minivan** · Seating capacity of up to eight passengers · Honda Odyssey, Kia Sedona, Toyota Sienna, Dodge Grand Caravan
Luxury premium car · Very comfortable and luxurious · Audi A8, BMW 750Li, Cadillac CT6	

B Identify the types of the following cars.

Vocabulary

Complete the following sentences by using the words from the box.

| brand new | brochure | compact | coverage | injury |
| insurance | mileage | pedestrians | performance | vehicle |

1 What's the license number of the _____?

2 This _____ has all the information about the product that you will need.

3 He suffered an _____ in a car accident.

4 Most major rental car companies allow drivers to have unlimited _____.

5 I prefer to rent a _____ car. Used cars are not safe.

6 We recommend you buy _____ when you rent a car.

7 The new SUV's _____ on mountain roads was impressive.

8 The number of people without insurance _____ increased last year.

9 I prefer driving a _____ car because of its small size.

10 While driving, you should pay attention to _____ who are crossing the street.

Listen Up

Listen to the dialogue and choose T (true) or F (false). 10-01

		T	F
1	The guest has a reservation to pick up a car.	☐	☐
2	The guest wants to rent a minivan.	☐	☐
3	The guest wants to rent a car for six people.	☐	☐
4	The rental car rate for a week is $330.	☐	☐
5	The guest thinks the rate is expensive.	☐	☐

Let's Talk ❶ Listen to the conversation and practice it with your partner. 🔊 10-02

Renting a Car

Guest	Excuse me. I'd like to rent a car. What kinds of cars do you have?
Rental Clerk	Here's a brochure. We have all types of cars. How many people are with you?
Guest	There are 4 of us. I want a full-size car which is safe and comfortable.
Rental Clerk	All our cars are in good condition. You'll be satisfied.
Guest	I hope so. What is the weekly rate for a full-size car?
Rental Clerk	Our rates start from $585 a week. That includes unlimited mileage and a full-coverage insurance plan.
Guest	I'll take this one, the Chevy Impala. It is $650 per week, right?
Rental Clerk	Yes, that's right. Could I have your driver's license and a credit card, please?

Role-Play

Practice the conversation with your partner again. Use the ideas in the box.

A	Excuse me. I'd like to rent a car. What kinds of cars do you have?
B	Here's a brochure. We have all types of cars. How many people are with you?
A	❶_____. I want a ❷_____ which is ❸_____.
B	All our cars are in good condition. You'll be satisfied.
A	I hope so. What is the weekly rate for a ❸_____?
B	Our rates start from $350 per week.
A	I'll take this one. It is ❹_____, right?
B	Yes, that's right. Could I have your driver's license and a credit card, please?

❶ Number of Passengers	❷ Class/Types of Car	❸ Reason for Choice	❹ Rental Condition
Just me	compact car	economical (fuel efficient)	$385 per week
My wife and I	midsize car	safe and comfortable (not expensive)	$412 per week
Three	SUV	good for off-road driving	$655 per week
Five including me	luxury full-size car	spacious	$825 per week
Seven	minivan	large enough for passengers and suitcases	$525 per week

Language Practice

A Make questions by using the words given.

What is	the rental charge the rate	for a week? for two weekdays? for a day? for the weekend?
How much is	it the full-size car the compact car	for two weeks? for three days? for four days?

1 rate / three weeks

2 rental charge / a month

3 micro-car / three days

4 minivan / five days

5 SUV / ten days

B Complete the following complex sentences by choosing the correct relative pronouns.

> I want somebody. He/she will help me.
> → I want somebody **who** will help me.
>
> I want to buy the coat. The coat fits me very well.
> → I want to buy the coat **which** fits me very well.
>
> I don't want something. It'll break down on the road.
> → I don't want something **that**'ll break down on the road.

1 I want to rent a car (who, which) is big and comfortable.

2 I don't want someone (who, which) hates me.

3 I want something (who, that) makes me feel good.

4 We need something (who, that) will last a long time.

5 He needs a box (who, that) can store his stuff.

Let's Talk ❷   Listen to the conversation and practice it with your partner. 🔊 10-03

Getting Lost in the City

Tourist	Excuse me, officer. Can you help me?
Police Officer	Sure. What can I do for you?
Tourist	I think I am lost. I have no idea where I am.
Police Officer	You are on 5th Avenue. Do you see Rockefeller Center over there?
Tourist	Yes, I do. How can I get to Times Square from here?
Police Officer	Go down this street until you see the New York Public Library.
Tourist	The New York Public Library. Okay. Then where should I go?
Police Officer	Turn right and go two blocks. You can find Times Square there. You can't miss it.

Role-Play

Practice the conversation with your partner again. Use the ideas in the box.

A Excuse me, officer. Can you help me?
B Sure. What can I do for you?
A I think I am lost. I have no idea where I am.
B You are ❶_____. Do you see ❷_____ over there?
A Yes, I do. How can I get to ❸_____?
B ❹_____.
A Okay. Then where should I go?
B ❺_____. You can find ❻_____ there. You can't miss it.

❶ Where You Are	❷ Landmark	❸ The Place to Go To	❹ First Directions	❺ Second Directions
on Jungang Street	City Hall	Jungang Elementary School	Go straight to the intersection	Turn left and then go one block
on Jong-no Street	the Kyobo Building	the Sejong Culture Center	Go down the street for three blocks	Turn right and go one block
in Millennium Park	Wal-Mart	the Chicago Tribune Building	Turn right at the corner	Go straight down Michigan Avenue

Language Practice

A Look at the different ways to ask for directions. Then, make questions by using the given words.

> **Where is** a convenience store around here?
> **Do you know where** the Staples Center is?
> **How can I get to** the Metropolitan Museum?
> **Could you tell me how to get to** Central Station?
> **Could you show me the way to** the post office?

1. how / I / get / Universal Studio

2. where / the nearest / gas station

3. tell / me / how / get / Tower Bridge

4. show / me / you / the / way / movie theater

5. do / know / where / Lincoln Memorial

B You can find these signs on U.S. roads and highways. Choose what each sign means from the box.

No Pedestrians	Bike Lane	Falling Rocks	No Right Turn
Right Turn	Stop	Deer-Crossing Area	Slippery Road
No Trucks	Do Not Enter		

1  2  3  4  5

6  7  8  9  10

Practice More

A Listen to the dialogue. Then, complete the following script. 🔊 10-04

Making a Reservation

Clerk	Good morning. Abiz Car Rental. How may I help you?
Tourist	I'd like to rent a car tomorrow morning.
Clerk	What ¹_____ would you like?
Tourist	A ²_____, please.
Clerk	I'm very sorry. There are no minivans ³_____ tomorrow.
Tourist	How about an SUV then?
Clerk	That's available tomorrow.

B Listen to the dialogue. Then, answer the following questions. 🔊 10-05

Gasoline Charge

1. What should the tourist do if he doesn't fill up the tank?
2. What is the rate for the extra gas charge?
3. Is the extra gas charge expensive?

C Listen to the dialogue. Then, put the following sentences in the correct order. 🔊 10-06

Giving Directions

1. You are on Madison Avenue. Go straight ahead and turn right at the second traffic light.
2. Excuse me. How can I get to the Empire State Building?
3. Thank you very much.
4. The Bank of America will be on your right. And the Empire State Building is next to it.

D Listen to the dialogue. Then, choose T (true) or F (false). 🔊 10-07

Asking for Directions	T	F
1 The tourist is looking for Lincoln Hospital.		
2 The Millennium Hilton Hotel is next to the Lincoln Museum.		
3 The tourist should go past the Bank of America to get to his destination.		

Wrap-Up

A Complete the sentences with the words or expressions you used in this unit.

ahead	choose	comfortable	fill ~ up	get to
idea	miss	purchase	rate	type

1. Could you please tell me how to _____ Times Square?
2. Do I have to _____ it _____ before I return it?
3. Do I have to _____ an insurance policy?
4. Go straight _____ and turn right at the second traffic light.
5. I have no _____ where I am.
6. I want a full-size car that is safe and _____.
7. We have all types and classes of cars you can _____ from.
8. What is the weekly _____ for a full-size car?
9. What _____ of car would you like, sir?
10. You can't _____ it.

B Look at how to rent a car online. What information do you need to make a reservation? Talk about it with your partner.

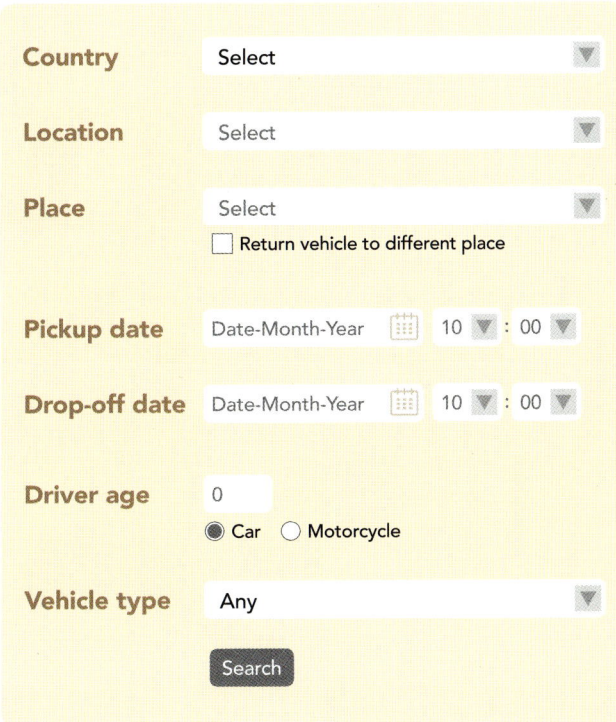

Unit 11

Are You Ready to Order?

In this unit, you will learn:
1. The different types of restaurants
2. Various foods on menus
3. How to order meals and to make complaints
4. How to pay the bill

Warm-Up

Look at the different types of restaurants. Then, choose the restaurant that you want to eat at. Answer the question and explain why you want to eat at that restaurant.

Casual-dining restaurants serve moderately priced food in a casual atmosphere.

Fine-dining restaurants provide high-quality services and high-priced food in an elegant atmosphere.

Fast-food restaurants or takeout restaurants expect the customer to order and collect the food at a counter.

A **cafeteria** is a type of food service location with no table service. Instead of table service, there are food-serving counters/stalls. Customers take the food they want as they walk along by placing it on a tray.

A **buffet** is a meal-serving system where customers serve themselves. It is a popular method of feeding large numbers of people with a minimal staff.

An **ethnic restaurant** specializes in ethnic or national cuisine. For example, Thai restaurants specialize in Thai cuisine.

> Where are you eating out tonight?

> I am going to a buffet. There are many different kinds of foods that I can choose.

1. Italian Restaurant. The appetizers there are really delicious.
2. French Restaurant. I'm dying to have some of the desserts there.
3. Korean Restaurant. The restaurant has the best service in town.

Vocabulary

Complete the following sentences by using the words from the box.

| cafeteria | clam chowder | complaint | correct | ethnic |
| rare | spicy | supposed to | take ~ order | take ~ out |

1 It will take some time to _____ all the mistakes.

2 A steak cooked _____ is mostly red and pink in the middle.

3 _____ food restaurants such as Thai, Vietnamese, Japanese, Italian, and Mexican are becoming popular in Korea.

4 If you have a _____ about our service, complete the customer service card.

5 May I _____ your _____, sir?

6 This dish is _____ be served warm.

7 What kind of soup do you prefer, _____ or cream of broccoli?

8 Are you going to eat here or _____ your meal _____?

9 The college _____ serves meals to students all throughout the day.

10 Korean food often has a very _____ taste.

Listen Up

Listen to the dialogue and choose T (true) or F (false).

		T	F
1	The name of the restaurant is Som Sack.	☐	☐
2	The guest has a reservation.	☐	☐
3	The guest needs a table for two.	☐	☐
4	The guest is seated in the nonsmoking section.	☐	☐
5	The guest wants a drink before ordering food.	☐	☐

Let's Talk ❶

Listen to the conversation and practice it with your partner.

Being Seated and Served

Waitress Good evening. Welcome to Joe's Restaurant. Do you have a reservation?

Guest Hello. I reserved a table for two tonight. The name is Sean Clark.

Waitress Ah, yes, Mr. Clark. A table for two at six in the nonsmoking section. Let me show you to your table, Mr. Clark. This way, please.

Guest Thank you. Could I have a menu, please?

Waitress Certainly, Mr. Clark. Here you are. Would you like to order a drink first?

Guest Yes. I will have a bottle of wine, please.

Waitress I'll be right back with your drink. Then, I will take your order.

Role-Play

Practice the conversation with your partner again. Use the ideas in the box.

A Good evening. Welcome to ❶_____ Restaurant. Do you have a reservation?

B Hello. I reserved a ❷_____. The name is Perry Martin.

A Ah, yes, Mr. Martin. A ❷_____ in the nonsmoking section. Let me show you to your table, Mr. Martin. This way, please.

B Thank you. Could I have a menu, please?

A Certainly, Mr. Martin. Here you are. Would you like to order a drink first?

B Sure. I will have ❸_____, please.

A I'll be back soon with your drink. Then, I will take your order.

❶ Name of the Restaurant	❷ Table and Reservation Time	❸ Drinks
Sullivan's	table for one at 6:30	mineral water
Eli's	table for three at 5:30	light beer
the Saloon	table for four at 5:00	cola
Gibson's	table for seven at 7:00	orange juice
Morton's	table for two at 7:30	soda

Language Practice

A Make sentences using "Let me."

Let me	show you to your table.
	show you to your room.
	take your bags to your room.
	tell you about today's specials.

1 tell / about / you / the soup of the day

2 give / some advice / you

3 tell / about my country / you

4 the reservation list / check

5 move / table / to another

6 myself / introduce / to you

B Look at the dialogue. Then, practice it with your partner by using the menu below.

> **A** Would you like to order a drink? / Would you like something to drink?
>
> **B** Yes. I'll have a bottle of beer, please.

Drinks

Herbal Tea
Green, Chamomile, Peppermint, Rooibos

Espresso

Americano

Cappuccino

Latte

Hot Chocolate

Milk

Juice
Orange, Pineapple, Cranberry, Tomato

Beer

Wine

Let's Talk ❷   Listen to the conversation and practice it with your partner. 🔊 11-03

Ordering Meals

Waitress	Are you ready to order, sir?
Guest	Yes. I'll have the New York steak, please.
Waitress	How would you like your steak, sir?
Guest	Medium rare, please.
Waitress	Okay. Would you like soup or salad with your meal?
Guest	I feel like some soup today. What is the soup of the day?
Waitress	We have two soups of the day: clam chowder and spicy chicken soup.
Guest	I will have the clam chowder, please.

Role-Play

Practice the conversation with your partner again. Use the ideas in the box.

A	Are you ready to order, sir?
B	Yes. I'll have the New York steak, please.
A	How would you like your steak, sir?
B	❶_____, please.
A	Okay. Would you like soup or salad with your meal?
B	I feel like some soup today. What is the soup of the day?
A	We have ❷_____.
B	I will have the ❷_____, please.

❶ How to Cook the Steak	❷ The Soup of the Day
rare	cream of broccoli
medium rare	tomato seafood soup
medium	chicken noodle soup
medium well	vegetable beef soup
well done	minestrone

Language Practice

A Make complaints using "too" and "It's supposed to be..."

> **Making Complaints**
>
> My soup is too cold. It's supposed to be warm.
>
> This table is too dirty. It's supposed to be clean.

1 this restaurant / noisy / quiet

2 this food / spicy / mild

3 this coffee / weak / strong

4 this soup / salty / bland

5 this movie / boring / exciting

6 this meat / rare / medium rare

B Make countersuggestions by using "I'm sorry. We don't…, but we do…" to your partner.

> **Making Countersuggestions**
>
> I'm sorry. We don't have any ocean trout left, but we do have some fresh Norwegian salmon.
>
> I'm sorry. We don't have any ice wine left, but we do have some other nice dessert wines.

1 cream of broccoli   minestrone   2 clam chowder   French onion soup

3 chocolate pudding   ice cream and a brownie   4 scrambled eggs   poached eggs and boiled eggs

5 apple juice   orange juice   6 salmon filet steak   teriyaki skirt steak

Practice More

A Listen to the dialogue. Then, complete the following script. 🔊 11-04

Visiting a Restaurant

Waiter	Good evening. Do you have a reservation?
Guest	No, I don't. Do you have a ¹_____ now?
Waiter	I'm very sorry. All our tables are ²_____ at the moment.
Guest	How long will we I have to wait for one?
Waiter	Around 30 minutes.
Guest	Thanks. I think I'll ³_____ another place.

B Listen to the dialogue. Then, answer the following questions. 🔊 11-05

The Way a Steak Is Cooked

1 How is the steak cooked?

2 How does the guest want his steak?

3 What will the waitress do?

C Listen to the dialogue. Then, put the following sentences in the correct order. 🔊 11-06

Mistaken Orders

1. I'm sorry for the mistake. I'll be back soon with your order.
2. I didn't order this salad. I ordered the soup of the day.
3. Thank you.
4. Yes. What can I do for you?
5. Excuse me.

D Listen to the dialogue. Then, choose T (true) or F (false). 🔊 11-07

Checking a Bill	T	F
1 There's something wrong with the credit card.		
2 The guest did not eat any dessert.		
3 The waiter did not apologize.		

Wrap-Up

A Complete the sentences with the words or expressions you used in this unit.

drink	have	left	order	ready
reservation	supposed	show	table for four	what

1 Do you have a _____?

2 I reserved a _____ in the nonsmoking section.

3 Let me _____ you to your table.

4 Would you like a _____ before your meal?

5 I'll _____ some orange juice, please.

6 I'll be back soon with your _____.

7 Are you _____ to order now?

8 The soup is too cold. It's _____ to be hot.

9 I'm sorry. We don't have any ice wine _____, but we do have some other nice dessert wines.

10 This salad is not _____ I ordered.

B Look at the menu below. Explain the menu to your guest and take orders.

MENU

APPETIZERS
- ROAST GARLIC WITH BREAD BASKET — $3.95
- ESCARGOT — $9.95
- FRIED CALAMARI — $9.95

SOUPS
- SOUP OF THE DAY — $3.95
- NEW ENGLAND CLAM CHOWDER — $4.95
- LENTIL SOUP — $4.95
- FRENCH ONION SOUP — $4.95

SALAD
- CAESAR SALAD — $7.95
- ROASTED RED PEPPER SALAD — $9.95
- GREEK SALAD — $12.95

MAIN COURSES
- BONELESS NEW YORK SIRLOIN — $34.95
- FILET MIGNON WITH PORTABELLO MUSHROOMS — $45.95
- ROAST PORK FILET — $29.95
- MARINADED CHICKEN BREAST — $34.95
- ALASKAN KING CRAB WITH WHITE TRUFFLES — $39.95
- CRISP PACIFIC COD AND BAKED OYSTERS — $29.95

DESSERT
- FRESHY FRUIT TART — $4.95
- NEW YORK STYLE CHEESECAKE — $4.95
- MIDNIGHT CHOCOLATE CAKE — $4.95
- BROWNIE PUDDING — $4.95
- TRIO OF SORBET — $5.95

More Useful Expressions

– I'll have the roast garlic with bread basket for an appetizer.
– We'd like lentil soup and French onion soup.
– Here are our main dishes.
– Here are our delicious dessert selections.
– What kinds of soup do you have?
– I'd like to start with an order of fried calamari.
– I'd love to have a bowl of New England clam chowder.
– I'll take a Caesar salad with ranch dressing.
– Let me have the marinated chicken breast.
– For my entrée, I'll have the roast pork filet.
– May I have a slice of midnight chocolate cake for dessert, please?

Unit 12
I Need a Present for My Parents

In this unit, you will learn:
1 About shopping places
2 How to get help from a sales clerk
3 How to ask about goods in different sizes, styles, and colors
4 How to get a refund

Warm-Up

A Read the descriptions of shops and decide where you should go shopping. Then, give reasons for your choice. Work with your partner.

- A **flea market**, often held outdoors, sells old and used articles, curios, and antiques.
- A **supermarket** sells various kinds of cheese, tea, meat, fresh fruit, and other goods.
- An **online shopping mall** typically has low prices and free shipping.
- A **farmers' market** has fresh fruits and vegetables sold directly by farmers to consumers.
- An **outlet mall** is a large group of shops that are directly run by manufacturers.
- A **department store** sells luxurious goods and has sections such as clothing, furniture, cosmetics, home appliances, sporting goods, and jewelry.
- A **convenience store** is open at all hours for the convenience of shoppers.
- A **drugstore** is a retail store where medicine and miscellaneous articles are sold.

> Where would you like to go shopping?

> I'd like to go to a farmers' market to buy some fresh fruits and vegetables directly from farmers.

B Where does each person want to go shopping?

convenience store	supermarket	outlet mall	department store

1 I want to buy a name-brand product at a cheap price.
2 I can buy some meat and cheese for sandwiches.
3 It is the only store open late at night.

Vocabulary

Complete the following sentences by using the words from the box.

| souvenir | receipt | gift-wrap | fitting room | exchange |
| refund | spend | discount | on sale | bargain |

1 I cannot _____ more than $20 a day on meals.

2 Club members can get a 20% _____.

3 You can get a full _____ within 30 days of purchase.

4 These items are _____ for just $9.99.

5 I bought a miniature of the Statue of Liberty as a _____ from New York.

6 My cousin bought a computer at a garage sale. It was a real _____.

7 Could you _____ this green shirt for a black one?

8 You need a _____ to get free parking at this shopping mall.

9 Could you _____ it with a pink ribbon?

10 Can I try it on? Where's the _____?

Listen Up

Listen to the dialogue and choose T (true) or F (false). 12-01

                                                                T   F

1 The customer is looking for a T-shirt.   ☐   ☐

2 The customer wants size 26.   ☐   ☐

3 The regular price of the item is 50 dollars.   ☐   ☐

4 The customer bought the dark green ones.   ☐   ☐

5 The customer is satisfied with the sale price.   ☐   ☐

Let's Talk ❶ Listen to the conversation and practice it with your partner. 12-02

Buying at a Clothing Store

Sales Clerk Good evening. Can I help you, sir?

Customer Yes, I need a present for my parents.

Sales Clerk Do you have anything particular in mind?

Customer I don't know. But I want to buy them something special.

Sales Clerk How about these dress shirts? These are very popular here.

Customer Do you have them in any other colors?

Sales Clerk Yes. We also have them in white, gray, and black.

Customer Are they on sale now?

Sales Clerk Yes, they are now 40 percent off the regular price.

Customer That's a real bargain. I'll take the white and gray ones.

Role-Play

Practice the conversation with your partner again. Use the ideas in the box.

A Good evening. Can I help you?

B Yes, I need a present for my ❶_____.

A Do you have anything particular in mind?

B I don't know. But I want to buy them something special.

A How about these ❷_____? These are ❸_____.

B Do you have them in any other colors?

A Yes. We also have them in ❹_____.

B Are they on sale now?

A Yes, they are now 40 percent off the regular price.

B That's a real bargain. I'll take the ❺_____.

❶ People	❷ Present	❸ Special Feature	❹ Colors	❺ Choice of Colors
sisters	sweaters	made of wool	ivory, orange, green, and pink	pink and orange ones
friends	football jerseys	genuine Manchester United jerseys	red, white, and blue	red one
grandparents	scarves	made of cashmere	gray, blue, and yellow	yellow and blue ones

Language Practice

A Look at the sample dialogues. Then, make questions and answers by using the words below.

Customer	Do you have them in any other colors?
Clerk	We have them in white, pink, yellow, orange, red, and purple.
Customer	Do you have this shirt in red or pink?
Clerk	We have some. But I'm sorry. The red ones are out of stock.
Customer	Do you have these shoes in size 8?
Clerk	Certainly, I'll get them for you.

Do you have _____ ?

_____ .

Customer	Clerk
this dress / size 4	Sure. / I'll get it for you.
these gloves / different sizes	Sorry. / only one size
that hat / black or white	Yes. / white
those pants / any other sizes	Yes. / small, medium, large
this suitcase / any other style	Sorry. / out of stock
that bag / different color	Yes. / blue, red

B Practice the dialogue with your partner. Use your own ideas for the reasons.

I want to buy perfume for my girlfriend because tomorrow is our 100th day anniversary.
I'll take these postcards for my brother because he collects souvenir postcards.

Items	For	Reason
perfume	sister	
postcards	brother	
hat / black or white	mother	
sweater	father	
leather shoes	best friend	

I Need a Present for My Parents

Let's Talk 2

Listen to the conversation and practice it with your partner. 12-03

Getting a Refund

Customer   Excuse me. I would like to return these sandals, please. I bought them yesterday.

Sales Clerk   Is there something wrong with them?

Customer   Yes, I like the color, but they don't fit very well.

Sales Clerk   Would you like to exchange them for another size?

Customer   No, thanks. The problem is not the size but the shape. I'd like to get a refund.

Sales Clerk   I see. I need the receipt and your credit card, please.

Customer   Here you are. Thank you for your help.

Sales Clerk   No problem.

Role-Play

Practice the conversation with your partner again. Use the ideas in the box.

A   Excuse me. I would like to return ❶_____, please. I bought ❷_____ yesterday.

B   Is there something wrong with ❷_____?

A   Yes, I like ❸_____, but I don't like ❹_____.

B   Would you like to exchange them for a different one?

A   No, thanks. I'd like to get a refund.

B   I see. I need the receipt and your credit card, please.

A   Here you are. Thank you for your help.

B   No problem.

❶ Item	❷ Pronoun	❸ Feature You Like	❹ Problem
this T-shirt	it	its color	its fabric
these shoes	them	their design	their color
this shoulder bag	it	its color	its design

Language Practice

A The following are a department store's sections. Suppose you are working at the information desk at this store. Please give the right directions to the customer. Make a conversation with your partner.

⟫⟫ 4F	**Brand Section**	Calvin Klein, Coach, DKNY, Guess, Levi's, Nike, Ralph Lauren, The North Face, Tommy Hilfiger, Clarks, Adidas, skin care, Ralph Lauren shirts, TVs, forks and spoons, slippers, stoves
⟫⟫ 3F	**Home Section**	bakeware, cookware, cutlery, silverware, glassware, mugs, tables, beds, sofas, chairs, dining room sets, dressers
	Home Appliances	refrigerators, washers & dryers, stoves, dishwashers, vacuums, TVs, audios
⟫ 2F	**Clothing Section**	dresses, coats, jackets, jeans, leggings, pants, shorts, sweaters, skirts, swimwear, tops, suits, socks
⟩ 1F	**Beauty Section**	makeup, skin care, fragrance, hair care, bath & body
	Jewelry	bracelets, diamonds, earrings, necklaces, rings, pearls
	Bags and Accessories	handbag brands, backpacks, wallets, luggage & travel
	Shoes	boots, comfort, heels, flats, sneakers, slippers, casual shoes, dress shoes

> Excuse me. I want to buy a <u>swimsuit</u>. Where should I go?

> You should go to the clothing section. It's on <u>the second floor</u>.

B Look at the sample dialogue. Then, practice it with your partner.

Clerk	Would you like to exchange it (them) for another color?
Customer	No. The problem is not the color but the shape.

1

2
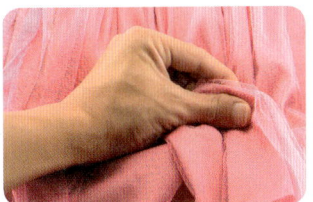

3

Practice More

A Listen to the dialogue. Then, complete the following script. 🔊 12-04

Price Bargaining

Customer	How much is this bag?
Sales Clerk	Let me check the price tag. It is ¹_____ dollars.
Customer	Could you give me a discount? It is out of my ²_____.
Sales Clerk	Sorry. We do not ³_____. Our prices are ⁴_____.
Customer	Okay. I'll ⁵_____ at some other places then.
Sales Clerk	Wait a minute! What price range do you have in ⁶_____?

B Listen to the dialogue. Then, answer the following questions. 🔊 12-05

Asking for Information

1 Where are the gift shops located?

2 How long does it take to get there?

3 What time do the shops close?

C Listen to the dialogue. Then, put the following sentences in the correct order. 🔊 12-06

Getting Help from a Sales Clerk

1. Sure. The fitting room is at the back of the store.
2. Absolutely gorgeous!
3. How about these shorts? They are very popular this summer.
4. Yes, I like the style. Can I try these on?
5. How do I look in these shorts?

D Listen to the dialogue. Then, choose T (true) or F (false). 🔊 12-07

Payment Methods	T	F
1 The customer bought it as a present.		
2 The total doesn't include tax.		
3 The store doesn't accept credit cards.		

Wrap-Up

A Complete the sentences with the words or expressions you used in this unit.

bargain	bring	cash	get	look
mind	off	tag	try on	wear

1. Can I _____ these navy blue jeans, please?
2. Do you have anything particular in _____?
3. We are offering a discount of 50 percent _____ the regular price.
4. It's a real _____.
5. Can I _____ a refund on these sandals, please?
6. Will you pay with _____ or by credit card?
7. Did you _____ the receipt?
8. What size do you usually _____?
9. Let me see the price _____. It is 189 dollars.
10. How do I _____ in these shorts?

B Answer the following questions. If you answer "Yes" to four or more of them, you may have a shopping problem. Share the results with your partner. Then, discuss your shopping habits.

	Yes	No
1. When I feel depressed, I usually go shopping.	☐	☐
2. I spend a lot of money on things I do not need.	☐	☐
3. I have closets full of clothes that I never wear.	☐	☐
4. I often feel out of control when I shop.	☐	☐
5. I lie to my friends and family about how much money I spend.	☐	☐
6. Even though I am worried about my debt, I still shop.	☐	☐
7. I feel upset and disturbed by my own shopping habits.	☐	☐
8. After a big shopping trip, I sometimes feel depressed.	☐	☐
9. My shopping has caused problems in my personal relationships.	☐	☐
10. If I can't buy something I really want, I feel very angry or upset.	☐	☐

Unit 13
I Want to See Some Sights in New York

In this unit, you will learn:
1. How to describe and recommend tourist attractions
2. How to ask for information about sightseeing
3. About various tourist attractions

Warm-Up

A The followings are the most-visited tourist attractions in New York City. Match the descriptions with the correct pictures.

a.

b.

c.

d.

e.

f.

g.

1. A commuter, rapid transit, and intercity railroad terminal at 42nd Street and Park Avenue in Midtown Manhattan
2. The most-visited urban park located in Manhattan, New York
3. A major commercial intersection, tourist destination, and entertainment center at the junction of Broadway and Seventh Avenue
4. Famous for its top-of-the-rock observation deck, skating on its iconic rink, NBC studio, and Christmas tree
5. An iconic symbol of freedom and of the United States as well as a gift from the French people to America
6. One of the oldest hybrid cable-stayed/suspension bridges between Manhattan and Brooklyn
7. A 102-story skyscraper located on Fifth Avenue and completed in 1931

B What city or country would you like to visit? Why do you want to go there? What tourist attractions are there? Talk to your partner.

> I'd like to visit London someday. London is the capital of the U.K., and there are many tourist attractions, such as Big Ben, Buckingham Palace, Westminster Abbey, the London Eye, and the British Museum. I can enjoy seeing new and old places in London.

Vocabulary

Complete the following sentences by using the words from the box.

| admission fee | allow | art gallery | balcony | depend |
| include | recommend | sightseeing | statues | tourist attractions |

1. Your travel expenses _____ on what you do while traveling.
2. Can you _____ a good Italian restaurant near here?
3. You don't have to pay an _____ to enter the museum.
4. Many hotels do not _____ people to bring their pets.
5. The museum has many _____ on display.
6. Paris has many popular _____ because it has been the capital of France for a long time.
7. The theater has 154 seats in the _____.
8. This _____ bus tour will let you explore uptown and downtown Manhattan.
9. The price does not _____ tax or a service charge.
10. A collection of paintings by Rene Magritte is on exhibition at the local _____.

Listen Up

Listen to the dialogue and choose T (true) or F (false). 13-01

		T	F
1	There are many tourist attractions in London.	☐	☐
2	The tourist is in New York now.	☐	☐
3	The tourist wants to visit some famous parks.	☐	☐
4	Regent Park is a ten-minute walk from the place where she is.	☐	☐
5	The tourist has to take a taxi to get to her destination.	☐	☐

Let's Talk ❶   Listen to the conversation and practice it with your partner. 🔊 13-02

A Trip to the Statue of Liberty

Tourist Pardon me. I want to see some sights in New York.

Official This brochure will help you.

Tourist Thank you. Would you recommend some good places to visit here in Manhattan?

Official Let me show you a few here in the brochure. The Statue of Liberty is good to visit in the morning. Or here, look. You shouldn't miss the Empire State Building, Times Square, Broadway, and Wall Street.

Tourist How can I get to the Statue of Liberty?

Official It is on Liberty Island. You should take a ferry to get there.

Tourist How long does the whole trip take?

Official It takes around three or four hours.

Role-Play

Practice the conversation with your partner again. Use the ideas in the box.

A Pardon me. I want to see some sights in New York.

B This brochure will help you.

A Thank you. Would you recommend some good places to visit?

B Let me show you a few here in the brochure. ❶_____ is good to visit. Or here, look. You shouldn't miss ❶_____.

A How can I get to ❶_____?

B You should take a ❷_____.

A How long does the whole trip take?

B It takes around ❸_____.

❶ Sites	❷ Transportation	❸ Duration
Times Square / Broadway, the Empire State Building	bus	five hours
the Brooklyn Bridge / Chinatown, Central Park	train	thirty minutes
Rockefeller Center / the Metropolitan Museum, Carnegie Hall	shuttle	one hour

Language Practice

A Look at the dialogue in the box. Imagine you live in the following cities. Give a tourist as much information as you can.

> Tourist Could you recommend some good places to visit here in New York?
>
> Official New York is full of interesting places to visit. Look. Here are the Empire State Building, Times Square, and the Metropolitan Museum. And you shouldn't miss the Broadway theaters.

1
Seoul

2
Tokyo

3
Paris

4
Sidney

Gyeongbokgung, Namdaemun Market, Lotte World, the World Cup Stadium, Namsan Seoul Tower

Odaiba, Roppongi Hills, Ueno Park, Meiji Shrine, Ginza

the Louvre Museum, Notre Dame Cathedral, the Eiffel Tower, the Pompidou Center, Montmarte Hill

the Opera House, the Harbor Bridge, Luna Park, Darling Harbor, the Queen Victoria Building

B You have to buy a MetroCard to use the subway in New York. Read the information about MetroCards. Then, complete the dialogue with your partner.

Single-Ride MetroCard
$2.00 for one subway or local bus ride with one free bus/bus transfer Single-Ride cards expire two hours after the time of purchase.

Pay-per-Ride MetroCards
$4.00 to $80.00 in any increment. Cards equal to or greater than $10.00 receive a 20% bonus.

Unlimited-Ride MetroCards
- Day Fun Pass: $7.00 for unlimited subway and local bus rides until 3 AM the day following first usage
- 7-Day Unlimited-Ride Card: $24.00 for unlimited subway and local bus rides until midnight seven days following first usage
- 30-Day Unlimited-Ride Card: $76.00 for unlimited subway and local bus rides until midnight thirty days following first usage

Tourist Excuse me. I'm not sure what kind of MetroCard I should purchase.

Official Okay. Are you planning to take the subway only once? In that case, you should buy _____.

Tourist Oh, no. I'm a tourist here. I'm going to be taking the subway and bus for a few days.

Official How long are you going to be here?

Tourist About one week.

Official In that case, you should buy _____. It costs $24.00 for unlimited rides for one week.

Tourist I see. I'll take one, please. Here is 24 dollars.

Official Thank you, and here is the card. Have a nice day.

Let's Talk 2

Listen to the conversation and practice it with your partner.

Helicopter Tour

Clerk	Good afternoon. What can I do for you?
Tourist	Hi. I'd like to get some information about the helicopter tour.
Clerk	Certainly, ma'am. What would you like to know?
Tourist	How much does it cost?
Clerk	It depends on the duration. A 10-minute tour will cost 350 dollars.
Tourist	What does that include?
Clerk	The price includes souvenir photos, a security fee, an insurance fee, and tax.
Tourist	I see. Where should I go to take the helicopter?
Clerk	Someone will pick you up at your hotel if you make a reservation.

Role-Play

Practice the conversation with your partner again. Use the ideas in the box.

A	Good afternoon. What can I do for you?
B	Hi. I'd like to get some information about the ❶_____.
A	Certainly. What would you like to know?
B	How much does it cost?
A	It depends on the duration. A ❷_____ tour will cost ❸_____.
B	What does that include?
A	The price includes ❹_____.
B	I see. Where should I go to take the ❺_____?
A	Someone will pick you up at your hotel if you make a reservation.

❶ Tour	❷ Duration	❸ Cost	❹ Services Included	❺ Transportation
city bus tour	three-hour	$65	a toll fee, a guide fee, and an admission fee	bus
submarine tour	one-hour	$90	a guide fee, a souvenir fee, and an insurance fee	submarine
hot-air balloon tour	two-hour	$115	a guide fee, a security fee, and an insurance fee	hot-air balloon

Language Practice

A Look at the dialogue. Then, make your own dialogue with your partner by using the information in the table below.

> Clerk   How much does it cost?
> Tourist   It depends on the _____. A(n) _____ will cost around _____.
>
> Clerk   What does the price include?
> Tourist   It includes _____.

Cost Depends On	Name of the Service Provided	Price	The Price Includes
type of car	mid-size car	$80 per day	full-coverage insurance and tax
type of room	double room	$250 per day	continental breakfast and swimming pool
class of seat	economy-class return ticket	$1,250	2 in-flight meals and tax, airport fee
duration and services provided	night-time cruise	$105	four-course dinner on deck and jazz band playing music for singing and dancing

B Practice the following dialogue pattern with your partner.

> **Tourist**
> Can you recommend some good places to see (visit)?
> Are there any good places you recommend?
>
> **Tourist Information Clerk**
> It's worth going to _____.
> I recommend _____.
> You should go to see _____.
> _____ shouldn't be missed.

1 St. Paul's Cathedral

2 Westminster Abby

3 Buckingham Palace

4 the London Eye

5 a River Thames boat tour

6 the Tower of London

Practice More

A Listen to the dialogue. Then, complete the following script. 🔊 13-04

Admission Fees

Tourist	How much is the ¹_____ fee?
Official	It's ²_____ for adults and ten dollars for students with a student ID. And children under ³_____ get in for free.
Tourist	Two adults and one child, please.
Official	Here are your tickets and ⁴_____ .

B Listen to the dialogue. Then, answer the following questions. 🔊 13-05

Asking Strangers for a Favor

1. What does the woman ask the man to do?
2. Why does the man say, "Cheese"?
3. Where does this kind of conversation most likely take place?

C Listen to the dialogue. Then, put the following sentences in the correct order. 🔊 13-06

Visiting a Museum

1. Oh, I see. One more question, please. Where is the gift shop around here?
2. Thank you. Is this brochure free?
3. Excuse me. Can I take a picture here?
4. Sorry. Taking pictures is not allowed here.
5. Yes, it is.
6. The museum shops are located on the first and second floors near the main entrance. You can buy some souvenirs there.

D Listen to the dialogue. Then, choose T (true) or F (false). 🔊 13-07

Ticket Reservations	T	F
1 The man is making a reservation for game tickets.		
2 There are no seats available in the balcony.		
3 Students can get a 20% discount.		

Wrap-Up

A Complete the sentences with the words or expressions you used in this unit.

| whole trip | depends on | sights | include | located |
| recommend | should | take | ten-minute walk | information |

1. Green Park is about a _____ from here.
2. I'd like to get some _____ about the tour.
3. I want to see some _____ in New York.
4. Would you please _____ a picture for us?
5. How long does the _____ take?
6. What does the price _____?
7. It _____ the duration. A 10- or 12-minute tour will cost around 350 dollars.
8. Where _____ I go to take the flight?
9. The museum shops are _____ on the first and second floors near the main entrance.
10. Could you _____ some good places to go?

B Read what tourist information centers usually provide. Then, talk about what information you want to get.

Tourist information centers usually provide
- information about tourist accommodations
- local maps, guidebooks, and brochures or leaflets about local events, entertainment, and tourist attractions
- bus/train/subway timetables
- opening and closing hours and admission charges for museums, historic sites, and art galleries

Official What can I do for you?
Tourist I want to know the business hours of the Italian restaurant.
Official It's open from 11:00 AM to 8:00 PM.
Tourist Thank you.

Listening Script

Unit 01 When Would You Like to Travel?

Listen Up

Agent Good morning. Koreana Air. How may I help you?

Passenger Hello. I would like to check on flights to New York for next week.

Agent When would you like to travel?

Passenger Well, I was thinking of next Tuesday, March 15.

Agent We have a few seats available on KA023. That flight leaves Incheon at 7:00 PM and arrives in New York at 1:30 PM the same day. Which class would you prefer?

Passenger I would like to reserve a business-class seat.

Agent All right. May I have your name, please?

Passenger Hines Ward.

Agent Could you spell your last name for me?

Passenger W-A-R-D.

Agent Could I have a contact number in Korea, please?

Passenger Sure. My business number is 795-2731, and my home number is 797-1234.

Agent Thank you. You are now confirmed in business class on KA023 going to New York on March 15. Your reservation number is 333-7777. Thank you for choosing Koreana Air. Have a nice day. Goodbye.

Let's Talk ❶ Flight Reservations

Agent Good morning. Koreana Air reservations. Jiyoon Lee speaking. How may I help you?

Passenger I'd like to reserve a round-trip ticket from Seoul to New York.

Agent Okay. When would you like to travel, sir?

Passenger I'd like to leave on June 15 and return on July 1. Are there any seats available?

Agent One moment, please. Let me check for you. Thank you for waiting, sir. How many people will be traveling?

Passenger I am traveling by myself.

Let's Talk ❷ Classes of Seats

Agent What class would you prefer?

Passenger I'd like to reserve a seat in business class.

Agent All right. May I have your name, please?

Passenger My name is Peter Philips.

Agent Could you spell your last name as it's written on your passport?

Passenger Sure. P-H-I-L-I-P-S.

Agent Thank you. Could I get your contact number in Korea, please?

Passenger Sure. My business number is 202-555-0165.

Agent Thank you very much for your cooperation.

Practice More

A *Canceling a Reservation*

Agent Good morning. Koreana Air Reservations. How may I help you?

Passenger I'd like to cancel my reservation on Flight 823 on the 23rd of this month.

Agent Sure. May I have your name, sir?

Passenger Tom Clause. C-L-A-U-S-E.

Agent One minute, please, Mr. Clause... Thank you for waiting. Your reservation is now canceled.

B *Calling about a Reservation*

Agent Hello, Koreana Air.

Passenger Hello. Is this the number for reservations?

Agent Yes, it is. How may I help you?

Passenger I made a reservation on the 10:20 flight to Tokyo on May 30, but I need to change my flight to June 1.

Agent May I have your name, please?

Passenger My last name is Casey. That's C-A-S-E-Y. And my first name is Patty.

Agent Wait a minute, please, Ms. Casey... Thank you for waiting. You are now confirmed on Flight KA703 to Tokyo on June 1.

C *Special Meal Requests*

Passenger Is it possible to request a vegetarian meal?

112

Agent	Certainly. May I have your reservation number, please?
Passenger	It's 953598.
Agent	Just a minute, please... Thank you for waiting. I have requested a vegetarian meal for you.

D Purchasing a Ticket

Passenger	I made a reservation last week, and I'd like to pay for my ticket now. My reservation number is 5513-2468.
Agent	One moment, please. Let me check... Thank you for waiting, Mr. Robert Johnson. You're going to Jakarta on March 23 on Flight KA627 and returning on April 10 on Flight KA628. You are flying in economy class. Is that correct?
Passenger	Yes, that's correct.
Agent	The total amount for your round-trip ticket comes to 814,400 won. Will that be cash or credit card?
Passenger	Cash.

Unit 02 May I See Your Ticket and Passport, Please?

Listen Up

1 Ladies and gentlemen, may I have your attention, please?
The Koreana Air check-in service has been temporarily stopped due to a computer system failure at John F. Kennedy Airport. We expect to start our check-in service in about 30 minutes. Please wait until we inform you again. We apologize for the inconvenience.

2 Ladies and gentlemen, may I have your attention, please?
We are very sorry to inform you that Koreana Air Flight 211 to Haneda has been delayed for about 2 hours and 30 minutes due to aircraft maintenance. We expect that the new departure time will be 10:30. We apologize deeply for the delay.

3 Ladies and gentlemen, may I have your attention, please?
Baggage security is now taking more time than usual. Passengers who have checked in their baggage, please wait about 10 minutes around near the screening. Then proceed to your departure gate for boarding. Thank you.

Let's Talk ❶ Flight Check-In

Agent	Good morning, sir. May I see your ticket and passport, please?
Passenger	Here you are.
Agent	Thank you. You are going to New York.
Passenger	Yes. Is the flight going to depart on time?
Agent	Yes, sir. The departure time is 10:40 AM. Do you have any baggage to check in?
Passenger	Yes, I have two suitcases.
Agent	Would you please put them on the scale?
Passenger	Sure.

Let's Talk ❷ Excess Baggage Charges

Agent	Excuse me, sir. You are going to New York via Tokyo. Are you aware of this, sir?
Passenger	Yes, I am. Can you through-check my bags to New York?
Agent	No problem, but your baggage is over the weight limit.
Passenger	Oh, really? Well, can't you just check them anyway?
Agent	I'm sorry, sir, but I have to charge you for the excess weight.
Passenger	Well, how much is that going to be?
Agent	It will be 200 U.S. dollars or 226,200 Korean won.
Passenger	Wow, that's quite expensive!

Practice More

A Passengers with Special Needs

Passenger	I asked one of your reservation agents to assist me at the airport.
Agent	Sure. What is your name and flight number?

Passenger My name is Christina Aguilera. I'm on Flight KA706.

Agent One moment, please. Miss Aguilera, a wheelchair is ready for you. Our agent will help you get on board.

B Passports 🔊 02-05

Agent Excuse me, sir. Your passport is not valid.

Passenger What? It can't be. Are you sure?

Agent Yes, sir. I'm sure. Do you by any chance have another passport?

Passenger No, I don't.

Agent Then I'm afraid you cannot travel to London.

Passenger I didn't realize that. What am I going to do? I really have to attend an important business meeting.

Agent Please contact your embassy, and perhaps they can give you an extension on your passport.

C Mileage Upgrades 🔊 02-06

Passenger I would like to use some of my miles to get an upgrade from economy to prestige class.

Agent May I have your SKYPASS card, please?

Passenger Oh, I don't have it with me.

Agent Don't worry, sir. May I have your date of birth?

Passenger April 10, 1987.

Agent Thank you. Within Southeast Asia, you need 15,000 miles to upgrade a round-trip ticket not during the peak season.

D Standby Passengers 🔊 02-07

Passenger I just heard your announcement looking for passengers willing to take the next flight to Osaka.

Agent Are you willing to wait, sir?

Passenger Sure, it's no problem.

Agent We appreciate your cooperation. May I see your ticket, please?

Passenger Here you are.

Agent Thank you, sir. Here is your MCO.

Passenger What's that?

Agent It's a compensation voucher for your trouble. It's valued at 30% of your airfare.

Unit 03 Would You Like a Window or Aisle Seat?

Listen Up 🔊 03-01

Agent Are you going to Los Angeles?

Passenger That's right. Is the flight going to depart on time?

Agent Yes, ma'am. The departure time is 10:40 AM. How many bags do you have?

Passenger Two suitcases.

Agent Would you like a window or aisle seat?

Passenger A window seat, please. At the front of the cabin.

Agent Okay, here are your boarding pass and baggage claim tags. Your seat number is 25A. You'll be boarding from Gate 19 at 10:10 AM.

Passenger Thank you. Where is the Member's Club lounge?

Agent It's upstairs on the third floor. Have a nice trip!

Passenger Thank you.

Let's Talk ❶ Seat Assignments 🔊 03-02

Agent Would you like a window or aisle seat?

Passenger Do you have a seat by the emergency exit?

Agent One moment, please. Are you traveling with anyone?

Passenger No, just me.

Agent Okay, your seat number is 12C. You'll be boarding from Gate 23 at 8:30 AM.

Passenger Thank you. Oh, where is a convenience store?

Agent There's one on the second floor. Thank you for flying on Koreana Air. Have a nice trip.

Passenger Thank you very much.

Let's Talk ❷ Security Screening 🔊 03-03

Security Personnel May I see your passport, please?

Passenger Here you go.

Security Personnel	Thank you. Would you please put your carry-on bag through the X-ray machine?
Passenger	Sure. Do I have to take off my jacket?
Security Personnel	Yes. And please put your laptop computer in the security bin.
Passenger	Okay. Can I carry this bottled water?
Security Personnel	No, you can't. Please proceed through the metal detector.
Passenger	All right. I'll have to throw away this water first.

Practice More

A Location of Lounges

Passenger	Excuse me. Where is the Morning Calm Lounge?
Agent	It's upstairs on the third floor. Just take the escalator on your left and then turn right. The signs will guide you.
Passenger	Where can I find the first-class lounge?
Agent	You can take the elevator at the end of the hall on the left to the third floor. The lounge will be on your left.

B Pre-Boarding Announcement

Passengers on Flight KA213 going to Paris, may I have your attention, please? This is to advise you that due to weather conditions, boarding will be delayed by about 30 minutes. Your new boarding time will be 11:30. We apologize for the inconvenience. Please wait at the boarding gate for further announcements. Thank you for your cooperation.

C Security Screening

Agent	Excuse me, ma'am. Would you please open your handbag?
Passenger	Is there a problem?
Agent	I'm afraid that your handbag contains an item that is not allowed on the flight.
Passenger	Oh, really? Let me open it for you to check.
Agent	Thank you, ma'am. This hand lotion is 180ml. You may return to the check-in counter and put it in your checked baggage. Otherwise, we need to confiscate it.

D Pre-Check-In Seat Assignment

Passenger	I'm flying in first class and would like to be assigned a seat.
Agent	Sure. May I have your reservation number?
Passenger	It's 171-7171. I'd like seat 1B, please.
Agent	All right. Let me check if the seat is still available. One moment, please. Thank you for waiting. Your seat has been assigned.

Unit 04 Welcome Aboard!

Listen Up

Ladies and gentlemen, may I have your attention please? We expect to begin boarding in approximately 5 minutes. In preparation for boarding, please listen carefully to the following announcement. To assist with boarding the aircraft, we ask passengers needing special assistance or passengers traveling with infants or young children to board first. We would then like to invite Koreana Air Morning Calm members and SkyTeam Elite members to board. And then economy-class passengers seated in rows 47 and higher are welcome to board.

Finally, all remaining economy-class passengers are welcome to board the aircraft. First- and prestige-class passengers, Koreana Air Million Miler and Morning Calm Premium members and SkyTeam Elite Plus members are welcome to board at their convenience through our Sky Priority lane. Boarding will commence shortly. Thank you for your cooperation.

Let's Talk ❶ Boarding

Cabin Crew Member	Good morning. Welcome aboard. May I see your boarding pass, please?
Passenger	Yes, here you are.
Cabin Crew Member	Thank you. Please take the aisle to the right. May I help you with your belongings?
Passenger	Yes, please. They're a bit heavy.

Listening Script **115**

Cabin Crew Member	Would you please put your bag under the seat in front of you?
Passenger	Can I put it in the overhead bin?
Cabin Crew Member	Oh, sure. Let me help you with it.
Passenger	Thank you so much!

Let's Talk ❷ Reading Material Service 🔊 04-03

Cabin Crew Member	Excuse me. Would you please fasten your seatbelt?
Passenger	Yes, of course. Could you give me another blanket and a pillow?
Cabin Crew Member	All right, sir. Please wait a moment while I get them.
Passenger	One more thing, please. Do you have any newspapers or magazines on the plane?
Cabin Crew Member	We have some fashion, business, and current events magazines and several newspapers.
Passenger	Can I have a *Sports Daily*?
Cabin Crew Member	I'm sorry, sir. We've run out of it. Would you like a *Sports Herald* instead?
Passenger	Yes, that would be great.

Practice More

A Seatbelts 🔊 04-04

Cabin Crew Member	Excuse me. Would you please fasten your seatbelt?
Passenger	I'm sorry. I don't know how to do that.
Cabin Crew Member	Oh, just pull it this way.
Passenger	Is this all right?
Cabin Crew Member	Sure. One more thing. Would you mind returning your seat to its upright position, please?
Passenger	Okay.

B Separated Passengers 🔊 04-05

Passenger	Excuse me, stewardess. My friend and I were assigned separate seats. Do you have any empty seats together?
Cabin Crew Member	I'll check for you... Thank you for waiting. There are some empty seats in the back of the cabin. Would that be all right, sir?
Passenger	Yes, that'll be fine. Thank you.

C Changing Seats 🔊 04-06

Passenger	Excuse me, stewardess. May I change seats?
Cabin Crew Member	Where would you like to sit, sir?
Passenger	In the front if possible.
Cabin Crew Member	I'm sorry, but I'm afraid there are no empty seats in the front. How about a seat in the middle of the cabin?
Passenger	No, thank you.

D Lavatory Information 🔊 04-07

Passenger	Excuse me. Can I use the lavatory now?
Cabin Crew Member	I'm sorry, sir. Would you mind using it after takeoff?
Passenger	I can't hold it.
Cabin Crew Member	Please hurry. We'll be taking off soon.

Unit 05 Would You Like Something to Drink?

Listen Up

Good morning, ladies and gentlemen.
On behalf of Captain Lee and the entire crew, welcome aboard Koreana Air, a member of SKYTEAM. This is Flight 607 bound for New York. This flight is a joint service operated by Koreana Air and Dell Airlines.
We are sorry for the delay. Our flight time to New

York will be 13 hours and 40 minutes. To prepare for takeoff, please turn off all portable electronic devices such as calculators and laptop computers until the seatbelt sign goes off. You may not use cellular phones, CD players, and radios at any time. Thank you for your cooperation and enjoy the flight.

Let's Talk ❶ Meal Service

Cabin Crew Member	Would you like something to drink? We have soda, juice, wine, and whiskey.
Passenger	Can I have some apple juice, please?
Cabin Crew Member	Here you are, sir. We have beef, fish, and *bibimbap* for dinner. What would you like to have?
Passenger	How is the fish cooked?
Cabin Crew Member	The fish is steamed in soy sauce. It is served with vegetables.
Passenger	I'll have the beef with some red wine, please.
Cabin Crew Member	Certainly, sir. Here you are and enjoy your meal!
Passenger	Thanks a lot.

Let's Talk ❷ In-Flight Duty-Free Sales

Cabin Crew Member	Would you like to buy any duty-free items?
Passenger	Yes, I want to buy a bottle of Chanel No. 5.
Cabin Crew Member	Certainly, sir. That'll be 142 dollars.
Passenger	Do you take Thai baht?
Cabin Crew Member	I'm sorry, but we don't. We only accept U.S. dollars, euros, and Korean won.
Passenger	Oh, I have some euros. How much is it in euros?
Cabin Crew Member	It's 121 euros and 30 cents.
Passenger	Here you are.
Cabin Crew Member	Thank you, sir. Here is your change.

Practice More

A Coffee Service

Cabin Crew Member	Would you like some coffee, sir?
Passenger	Yes, please.
Cabin Crew Member	Place your cup on the tray, please. Thank you, sir. Do you need any cream or sugar?
Passenger	Cream only.
Cabin Crew Member	It's extremely hot. Please be careful.

B Meal Service

Cabin Crew Member	Excuse me, sir. Have you finished your meal?
Passenger	Yes, I'm finished.
Cabin Crew Member	May I take your meal tray, sir?
Passenger	Yes, please.
Cabin Crew Member	I hope you enjoyed your meal, sir.
Passenger	Oh, thank you. It was delicious.
Cabin Crew Member	I'm glad to hear that.

C Passenger Requests

Passenger	Can you tell me what *bibimbap* is?
Cabin Crew Member	Sure. It's a Korean rice dish served with seasoned vegetables, ground beef, and a sauce.
Passenger	Okay, I'll try that.
Cabin Crew Member	Here's the *bibimbap*. You can add the sesame oil and *gochujang* that are on the tray. *Gochujang* is a Korean red chili paste. It can be spicy, so just add a little at a time.
Passenger	Thank you. It looks delicious!

D Handling a Sick Passenger

Passenger	Excuse me. I don't feel very well.
Cabin Crew Member	What's the matter, sir?
Passenger	I think I have airsickness. Can I have some medicine?
Cabin Crew Member	Sure. We have some airsickness pills. Would that be okay?
Passenger	Yes, please.

Unit 06 What's the Purpose of Your Visit?

Listen Up

Ladies and gentlemen, we will be landing shortly. Please fasten your seatbelts, return your seats and tray tables to the upright position, and open your window shades. In addition, please place large electronic devices such as laptop computers under your seats or in the overhead bins. For those connecting to other flights, here are some gate numbers for you. Flight 21 for Dallas is departing from Gate 11. Flight 193 for Chicago is leaving from Gate 7. And Flight 76 for Denver is leaving from Gate 14. Thank you.

Let's Talk ❶ Immigration

Official	Good morning. May I see your passport, please?
Passenger	Here you are.
Official	What's the purpose of your visit?
Passenger	I'm here to study English.
Official	I see. How long are you going to stay in the United States?
Passenger	I'm planning to stay here for about 10 months.
Official	Okay. Where will you be staying?
Passenger	I will be staying with a host family. I'm doing a homestay.

Let's Talk ❷ Customs Inspection

Official	Do you have anything to declare?
Passenger	No, I have nothing to declare.
Official	Do you have any fruits, plants, vegetables, or meat?
Passenger	No, I don't. But I have some wine.
Official	How much wine do you have?
Passenger	I only have a bottle.
Official	That's okay. Do you have more than 10,000 U.S. dollars?
Passenger	No, I don't. I only have 300 U.S. dollars.
Official	No problem. Please proceed to the exit marked "Nothing to Declare."
Passenger	Thanks. I appreciate it.

Practice More

A Immigration Inspection

Official	Passport and forms, please.
Passenger	Here you are.
Official	Place your index finger on the scanner, please.
Passenger	Here?
Official	Yes. Thank you. And look into the camera, please.
Passenger	This one?
Official	Yes. Hold on a moment, please.
Passenger	Is it finished?
Official	Yes, that's good. Thank you.

B Transit Passenger Information

Passenger	Excuse me. I'm looking for the Delta counter. Can you tell me where it is?
Official	Sure. It's in Terminal 2. Are you connecting to Delta?
Passenger	Yes, I am. Could you tell me if Flight 835 to Orlando has departed yet?
Official	I'm terribly sorry, ma'am. Flight 835 to Orlando departed 15 minutes ago.
Passenger	Oh, no. I have to get there by tomorrow afternoon.
Official	Well, the next available flight to Orlando is Delta Airlines Flight 723. It leaves at 8:30 PM.
Passenger	Okay. Could you reserve a seat on the flight for me?
Official	Sure. May I have your name, please?

C Terminal Information

Passenger	Where is the Delta counter?
Official	It's in Terminal 2.
Passenger	How can I get to Terminal 2?
Official	Take the shuttle bus on the second floor and get off at the first stop. The Delta counter is on the third floor.
Passenger	Thank you very much.

D Customs Inspection

Official	Do you have anything to declare?
Passenger	Yes. I have a carton of cigarettes.
Official	Could you open your bag, please?
Passenger	Oh, no.
Official	What are these small boxes? You didn't mention anything about these watches.
Passenger	Those are gifts.

Unit 07 My Baggage Is Missing

Listen Up

Ladies and gentlemen, may I have your attention please?
Baggage of a similar size, shape, or color may be easily mistaken for another passenger's baggage. Please identify each piece of baggage by the check-in tag number and identification.

Passenger	Excuse me. Are there any bags left to be loaded on the conveyor?
Airport Personnel	I'm sorry, ma'am. There are no more bags for this carousel. Is there a problem?
Passenger	I couldn't find my baggage.
Airport Personnel	Which flight did you arrive on?
Passenger	I just got off the Delta Airlines flight from New York.
Airport Personnel	Why don't you go to the lost and found office and fill out a property irregularity report?
Passenger	I don't understand why my bags didn't make it. Where is the lost and found office?
Airport Personnel	It's next to Carousel 1.
Passenger	Thank you.

Let's Talk ❶ Lost and Found

Passenger	Excuse me. I've just arrived from New York, but my baggage is missing.
Official	May I see your baggage claim tag and your boarding pass, please?
Passenger	Yes, here they are.
Official	Would you fill out this form while we trace your baggage?
Passenger	I'm really upset. What happened to my bag?
Official	I am sorry for the inconvenience. Your baggage will arrive on the next flight from New York.
Passenger	Should I collect my baggage here?
Official	No. We will deliver it to your address.

Let's Talk ❷ Baggage Claim

Official	How many bags are you missing?
Passenger	Just one. I need it before 9 AM.
Official	Okay. Could you please describe it for me?
Passenger	Sure. It's a regular black suitcase with two wheels.
Official	What size is it?
Passenger	It's medium sized. When can I get my bag?
Official	We will contact you as soon as we find it.
Passenger	Please hurry. I need my suit for a conference meeting.

Practice More

A Baggage Claim Information

Passenger	Excuse me. Could you please tell me where I can pick up my bags?
Official	Certainly. Which flight did you arrive on?
Passenger	I came from Seoul, Korea. I don't know the flight number.
Official	No problem. Were you traveling on Koreana Air?
Passenger	That's right.
Official	Then you can pick up your baggage at Carousel number 11.

B Delayed Baggage

Passenger	Where can I pick up my delayed bags?
Official	If you leave your address and contact number here, we can forward your bags to you as soon as possible.

Passenger	Great. Thank you.	Guest	What's the room rate for that period?
Official	Would you please sign this property irregularity report?	FDC	It's $185 per night.
Passenger	Sure.	Guest	Okay, I'd like to make a reservation.

C Lost Baggage 🔊 07-06

Passenger Can you tell me what happened to my lost bags?

Official We haven't received any information from the airport you departed from. I recommend filling out a lost-and-found form.

Passenger I don't understand why my bags didn't make it.

Official We apologize for any inconvenience this has caused you.

D Baggage Complaints 🔊 07-07

Passenger Excuse me. I have a complaint.

Official What seems to be the problem?

Passenger My suitcase has been completely destroyed. I want to be compensated.

Official I see. Please fill out this form. Indicate the damage caused and the value of the suitcase.

Unit 08 I'd Like a Double Room with an Ocean View

Listen Up 🔊 08-01

Front Desk Clerk Hello. Amicable Hotel reservation desk. Lee speaking. How may I help you?

Guest Hello. I'd like to book a room for September 21.

FDC How long will you be staying, sir?

Guest I'd like to stay for three nights.

FDC What type of room would you like, sir?

Guest A double room with a bath, please.

FDC We have double rooms available on the 15th floor.

Let's Talk ❶ Hotel Reservation 🔊 08-02

Receptionist Good morning. Manhattan Hotel reservations. Lee speaking. How may I help you?

Guest Hello. I'd like to book a room from June 4. Do you have any vacancies?

Receptionist Yes, sir. We have several rooms available on that day. How long will you be staying?

Guest I'll be staying for two nights.

Receptionist How many people will be with you?

Guest There will be two of us. I'd like a double room with an ocean view.

Receptionist Great. May I have your name and contact number, please?

Guest I'm Chuck Stockman, and my cell phone number is 773-246-4554.

Receptionist All right, Mr. Stockman. Your reservation has been made for a double room with an ocean view for two nights from June 4.

Guest Perfect. Thank you so much.

Let's Talk ❷ Hotel Check-In 🔊 08-03

Receptionist Good afternoon, sir and madam. How may I help you?

Guest I have a reservation. My name is Chuck Stockman.

Receptionist Thank you, Mr. Stockman. Yes, you have a double room with an ocean view for two nights.

Guest That's right. I want my room to be located on a high floor.

Receptionist Yes, your room is on the fifteenth floor. It's room 1505. Here is your key card.

Guest Thank you.

Receptionist Please fill out this registration card and sign here.

Guest   Sure. Where is the elevator?
Receptionist The elevators are on your right next to the gift shop. Enjoy your stay.

Practice More

A No Rooms Available

FDC   Good morning. Hyatt Reservation Desk. Susan speaking. Can I help you?
Guest Yes. Do you have a twin room available for tomorrow night?
FDC   Sorry. We are fully booked for tomorrow night.
Guest How about a double room?
FDC   I'm sorry, sir. It's the peak season now.
Guest Oh, that's disappointing. Well, thank you anyway.

B Changing Your Reservation

FDC   Your room number is 206. It's on the second floor.
Guest Could you change it to a room higher than the 15th floor, please?
FDC   Sorry, but that's not possible. The rooms on the higher floors are all occupied.
Guest How about a room on the 7th or 8th floor?
FDC   Let me check. Yes, there are a couple of rooms left on the 7th floor.
Guest Okay, I'll take one.

C Smoking or Nonsmoking?

FDC   Good afternoon. May I help you?
Guest Do you have a room available for tonight? I have no reservation.
FDC   How long will you be staying?
Guest Three nights.
FDC   Just a minute, ma'am. We only have smoking rooms left. Is that okay with you?
Guest No, thanks. I don't like smoking rooms.

D Different Room Rates

FDC   What kind of room would you like, ma'am?
Guest I'd like a double room with an ocean view, please.
FDC   There's an additional charge for a room with an ocean view. Is that okay?
Guest How much is the additional charge?
FDC   The additional charge is $30.00 per night. So the total rate will be $210.00 per night.
Guest That's quite expensive.

Unit 09 We Have a Business Center on the Second Floor

Listen Up

Guest   Hello. I'm a guest here.
Concierge   Hello. How may I help you?
Guest   Is there a gift shop in this hotel?
Concierge   Yes. We have a couple of gift shops here. One is on the ground floor over there, and the other is in the basement.
Guest   Thank you. Do you also have a fitness club or a swimming pool?
Concierge   Yes, ma'am. We have a fitness club on the second floor and a swimming pool on the second basement level right next to the indoor golf club.
Guest   One more question. Where is the bar?
Concierge   It's on the top floor.
Guest   Thank you very much.

Let's Talk ❶ Complaints and Requests

Receptionist Hello. Front Desk. How may I help you?
Guest   Hi. This is room 902. I have a problem with the bathroom. There is no hot water.
Receptionist Oh, I'm very sorry, sir. I'll send someone up right away.
Guest   And could you help me out with something else? Where is the business center?
Receptionist The business center is on the second floor.

Guest	Thank you. One more thing. Could you please give me a wakeup call at 6:45 tomorrow morning?
Receptionist	Certainly. A wakeup call at 6:45 for room 902.
Guest	That's correct. Thank you.

Let's Talk ❷ Checking Out 🔊 09-03

Guest	Can I check out now? My name is Patrick Hill, and I'm in room 816. Here is the key card.
Receptionist	Thank you. Just a moment, please. I'll get your bill... Here you are, Mr. Hill. Your total is $525.75. That includes service charge and tax. Please check to see if everything is correct.
Guest	Let me see... I think it's all right.
Receptionist	How would you like to pay?
Guest	By credit card. Is that okay?
Receptionist	Certainly. Here is your receipt. I hope you enjoyed staying with us.
Guest	I had an excellent stay. Thank you.

Practice More

A Guest Room Equipment 🔊 09-04

Bellhop	Here you are, Ms. Kim. This is your room.
Ms. Kim	Wow. It's very nice. But it's a little hot and humid in here.
Bellhop	We have air conditioning. Turn the switch clockwise to make the temperature cooler.
Ms. Kim	Where's the refrigerator?
Bellhop	It's right here. And this bottled water is complimentary.
Ms. Kim	Okay. Thank you very much.

B Making Complaints about Hotel Rooms 🔊 09-05

Clerk	Hello. Front Desk. How may I help you?
Guest	This is room 525. There's something wrong with the TV. I can't turn it on.
Clerk	I'm sorry. I'll have it checked out for you.
Guest	Please hurry. The Super Bowl starts in 20 minutes.

C Asking to Keep Baggage 🔊 09-06

Guest	Excuse me. Can I ask you for a favor?
Concierge	Sure. How may I help you?
Guest	Could you keep my suitcases for a couple of hours?
Concierge	What is your room number?
Guest	Room 2012. But I just checked out.
Concierge	No problem. Take this tag with you. You need the tag when you reclaim them.

D Correcting Mistakes 🔊 09-07

Receptionist	Here's your bill, Mr. Yang.
Guest	Um... I think there is a mistake on my bill. Could you please explain this item?
Receptionist	Let me check. It's your international call charge.
Guest	Really? I didn't make any overseas calls from my room.
Receptionist	Did you use the fax machine in the business center?
Guest	No.
Receptionist	I am sorry for the mistake. I'll check again and remove this item right away.

Unit 10 What Kinds of Cars Do You Have?

Listen Up 🔊 10-01

Guest	Excuse me. I'd like to rent a car. What kinds of cars do you have?
Clerk	Here's a brochure for you. We have all types and classes of cars you can choose from. For how many people?
Guest	Six including me. I want a minivan which is in good condition.
Clerk	Don't worry about that. All our cars are brand new. You'll be satisfied.
Guest	I hope so. What is the weekly rate for a minivan with full-coverage insurance?

Clerk   Our rates start at $625 a week.

Guest   Oh, that's quite expensive. Are there any other choices?

Let's Talk ❶ Renting a Car

Guest   Excuse me. I'd like to rent a car. What kinds of cars do you have?

Rental Clerk   Here's a brochure. We have all types of cars. How many people are with you?

Guest   There are 4 of us. I want a full-size car which is safe and comfortable.

Rental Clerk   All our cars are in good condition. You'll be satisfied.

Guest   I hope so. What is the weekly rate for a full-size car?

Rental Clerk   Our rates start from $585 a week. That includes unlimited mileage and a full-coverage insurance plan.

Guest   I'll take this one, the Chevy Impala. It is $650 per week, right?

Rental Clerk   Yes, that's right. Could I have your driver's license and a credit card, please?

Let's Talk ❷ Getting Lost in the City

Tourist   Excuse me, officer. Can you help me?

Police Officer   Sure. What can I do for you?

Tourist   I think I am lost. I have no idea where I am.

Police Officer   You are on 5th Avenue. Do you see Rockefeller Center over there?

Tourist   Yes, I do. How can I get to Times Square from here?

Police Officer   Go down this street until you see the New York Public Library.

Tourist   The New York Public Library. Okay. Then where should I go?

Police Officer   Turn right and go two blocks. You can find Times Square there. You can't miss it.

Practice More

A Making a Reservation

Clerk   Good morning. Abiz Car Rental. How may I help you?

Tourist   I'd like to rent a car tomorrow morning.

Clerk   What type of car would you like?

Tourist   A minivan, please.

Clerk   I'm very sorry. There are no minivans available tomorrow.

Tourist   How about an SUV then?

Clerk   That's available tomorrow.

B Gasoline Charge

Tourist   Do I have to pay for gas?

Clerk   No, your car is full of gas now.

Tourist   Then do I have to fill it up before I return it?

Clerk   That's right. If you don't fill up the tank, you'll have to pay an extra gas charge.

Tourist   How much is the charge?

Clerk   We charge $3.50 per gallon. It's a little higher than the pump price.

Tourist   A little? That's almost double the pump price.

C Giving Directions

Tourist   Excuse me. How can I get to the Empire State Building?

Official   You are on Madison Avenue. Go straight ahead and turn right at the second traffic light. The Bank of America will be on your right. And the Empire State Building is next to it.

Tourist   Thank you very much.

D Asking for Directions

Tourist   Excuse me, sir. How do I get to the Millennium Hilton Hotel?

Official   We are on Marina Drive now. Go straight two blocks and turn right onto Church Road.

Tourist   Go two blocks and turn right onto Church Road. And then?

Official   Go past the Bank of America and cross Victoria Street.

Tourist	The Bank of America and Victoria Street. After that?
Official	Go two more blocks along Church Road, and you'll see the Millennium Hilton Hotel on your right next to the Lincoln Museum. You can't miss it.

Unit 11 Are You Ready to Order?

Listen Up

Waitress	Good evening. Welcome to Som Sack.
Guest	Hello. I reserved a table for four for six o'clock. The last name is Roland.
Waitress	Ah, yes, Mr. Roland. A table for four at six. Would you like smoking or nonsmoking?
Guest	Smoking seats, please.
Waitress	All right. Let me show you to your table, Mr. Roland. This way, please.
Guest	Thank you.
Waitress	Here is the menu. Today's specials are green curry and ginger chicken. Would you like to order a drink first?
Guest	Sure. We'll have a couple of beers, please.
Waitress	I'll be back soon with your drinks. Then, I will take your order.

Let's Talk ❶ Being Seated and Served

Waitress	Good evening. Welcome to Joe's Restaurant. Do you have a reservation?
Guest	Hello. I reserved a table for two tonight. The name is Sean Clark.
Waitress	Ah, yes, Mr. Clark. A table for two at six in the nonsmoking section. Let me show you to your table, Mr. Clark. This way, please.
Guest	Thank you. Could I have a menu, please?
Waitress	Certainly, Mr. Clark. Here you are. Would you like to order a drink first?
Guest	Yes. I will have a bottle of wine, please.
Waitress	I'll be right back with your drink. Then, I will take your order.

Let's Talk ❷ Ordering Meals

Waitress	Are you ready to order, sir?
Guest	Yes. I'll have the New York steak, please.
Waitress	How would you like your steak, sir?
Guest	Medium rare, please.
Waitress	Okay. Would you like soup or salad with your meal?
Guest	I feel like some soup today. What is the soup of the day?
Waitress	We have two soups of the day: clam chowder and spicy chicken soup.
Guest	I will have the clam chowder, please.

Practice More

A Visiting a Restaurant

Waiter	Good evening. Do you have a reservation?
Guest	No, I don't. Do you have a table for three now?
Waiter	I'm very sorry. All our tables are taken at the moment.
Guest	How long will we have to wait for one?
Waiter	Around 30 minutes.
Guest	Thanks. I think I'll try another place.

B The Way a Steak Is Cooked

Guest	Excuse me.
Waitress	Yes? Is there anything wrong, sir?
Guest	My steak is too rare. It is supposed to be medium.
Waitress	I'm sorry, sir. I'll take it back to the kitchen and bring you another one. Anything else?
Guest	Can I get some more water?
Waitress	Sure.

C Mistaken Orders

Guest	Excuse me.
Waiter	Yes. What can I do for you?
Guest	I didn't order this salad. I ordered the soup of the day.

Waiter	I'm sorry for the mistake. I'll be back soon with your order.
Guest	Thank you.

D Checking a Bill

Guest	May I have the bill, please?
Waiter	Yes, of course. Here you are.
Guest	Excuse me. What's this on the bill?
Waiter	It's for your dessert.
Guest	I didn't have any dessert.
Waiter	I'm very sorry. I'll correct it right away.

Unit 12 I Need a Present for My Parents

Listen Up

Sales Clerk	Can I help you find something, ma'am?
Customer	Yes, do you have jeans in size 26?
Sales Clerk	Certainly. They're over here.
Customer	Do you have them in any other colors?
Sales Clerk	Yes, we have them in black, navy blue, dark green, and charcoal gray.
Customer	Can I try on these jeans, please?
Sales Clerk	Sure. The fitting rooms are over there at the end of this aisle.
Customer	How much are they?
Sales Clerk	Normally, they are 100 dollars.
Customer	One hundred dollars! That's expensive.
Sales Clerk	Well, they are on sale now. If you buy one, you can get another one free.
Customer	Wow, that's a real bargain. I'll take the black ones and the navy blue ones.

Let's Talk ❶ Buying at a Clothing Store

Sales Clerk	Good evening. Can I help you, sir?
Customer	Yes, I need a present for my parents.
Sales Clerk	Do you have anything particular in mind?
Customer	I don't know. But I want to buy them something special.
Sales Clerk	How about these dress shirts? These are very popular here.
Customer	Do you have them in any other colors?
Sales Clerk	Yes. We also have them in white, gray, and black.
Customer	Are they on sale now?
Sales Clerk	Yes, they are now 40 percent off the regular price.
Customer	That's a real bargain. I'll take the white and gray ones.

Let's Talk ❷ Getting a Refund

Customer	Excuse me. I would like to return these sandals, please. I bought them yesterday.
Sales Clerk	Is there something wrong with them?
Customer	Yes, I like the color, but they don't fit very well.
Sales Clerk	Would you like to exchange them for another size?
Customer	No, thanks. The problem is not the size but the shape. I'd like to get a refund.
Sales Clerk	I see. I need the receipt and your credit card, please.
Customer	Here you are. Thank you for your help.
Sales Clerk	No problem.

Practice More

A Price Bargaining

Customer	How much is this bag?
Sales Clerk	Let me check the price tag. It is 189 dollars.
Customer	Could you give me a discount? It is out of my price range.
Sales Clerk	Sorry. We do not bargain. Our prices are fixed.
Customer	Okay. I'll look around at some other places then.
Sales Clerk	Wait a minute! What price range do you have in mind?

B Asking for Information

Tourist	Excuse me. Can you tell me where I can buy some souvenirs?

Pedestrian	Well, there are some nice gift shops on Lincoln Street. It's about a five-minute walk from here.
Tourist	What are their business hours?
Pedestrian	They are open from 9:00 AM to 8:00 PM.

C Getting Help from a Sales Clerk

Sales Clerk	How about these shorts? They are very popular this summer.
Customer	Yes, I like the style. Can I try these on?
Sales Clerk	Sure. The fitting room is at the back of the store.
Customer	How do I look in these shorts?
Sales Clerk	Absolutely gorgeous!

D Payment Methods

Customer	Could you gift-wrap it, please? How much is the total?
Sales Clerk	One hundred and twenty-five dollars and seventy-five cents, including tax. Will you pay with cash or by credit card?
Customer	Do you accept Visa?
Sales Clerk	Sure.

Unit 13 I Want to See Some Sights in New York

Listen Up

Tourist	Excuse me. Can you recommend the best places to visit in London?
Official	Well, London has many great places to visit. There are palaces, theaters, shopping streets, parks, and museums. Which places are you interested in?
Tourist	Well, how about parks? I'd like to visit some famous parks.
Official	Actually, there are many famous parks in London. Look at this map. Green Park, St. James Park, Hyde Park, and Kensington Gardens are in the center of the city.
Tourist	How can I get to Green Park?
Official	It is only a ten-minute walk from here. You can either walk or take the tube or a bus to reach the other parks.
Tourist	Thank you so much.
Official	You're welcome. Have a nice day!

Let's Talk ❶ A Trip to the Statue of Liberty

Tourist	Pardon me. I want to see some sights in New York.
Official	This brochure will help you.
Tourist	Thank you. Would you recommend some good places to visit here in Manhattan?
Official	Let me show you a few here in the brochure. The Statue of Liberty is good to visit in the morning. Or here, look. You shouldn't miss the Empire State Building, Times Square, Broadway, and Wall Street.
Tourist	How can I get to the Statue of Liberty?
Official	It is on Liberty Island. You should take a ferry to get there.
Tourist	How long does the whole trip take?
Official	It takes around three or four hours.

Let's Talk ❷ Helicopter Tour

Clerk	Good afternoon. What can I do for you?
Tourist	Hi. I'd like to get some information about the helicopter tour.
Clerk	Certainly, ma'am. What would you like to know?
Tourist	How much does it cost?
Clerk	It depends on the duration. A 10-minute tour will cost 350 dollars.
Tourist	What does that include?
Clerk	The price includes souvenir photos, a security fee, an insurance fee, and tax.
Tourist	I see. Where should I go to take the helicopter?
Clerk	Someone will pick you up at your hotel if you make a reservation.

Practice More

A Admission Fees 🔊 13-04

Tourist How much is the admission fee?

Official It's twenty dollars for adults and ten dollars for students with a student ID. And children under twelve get in for free.

Tourist Two adults and one child, please.

Official Here are your tickets and change.

B Asking Strangers for a Favor 🔊 13-05

Woman Excuse me. Would you please take a picture for us?

Man Sure. Which button should I press?

Woman This one. Press it until you hear the click.

Man Okay. Say, "Cheese." One, two, three!

C Visiting a Museum 🔊 13-06

Tourist Excuse me. Can I take a picture here?

Security Sorry. Taking pictures is not allowed here.

Tourist Oh, I see. One more question, please. Where is the gift shop around here?

Security The museum shops are located on the first and second floors near the main entrance. You can buy some souvenirs there.

Tourist Thank you. Is this brochure free?

Security Yes, it is.

D Ticket Reservations 🔊 13-07

Tourist I'd like to reserve two tickets to the *Phantom of the Opera* for Sunday night.

Clerk What seats would you like?

Tourist Balcony seats, please.

Clerk Sorry. No seats are left in the balcony. But there are some seats available in the front row stalls.

Tourist Is there a student discount?

Clerk Yes, tickets are 25% off with a student ID.

Answer Key

Unit 01 When Would You Like to Travel?

Vocabulary p. 9

1 departure
2 round-trip
3 available
4 confirm
5 airfare
6 reservation
7 destination
8 prefer
9 passengers
10 request

Listen Up

1 T
2 F
3 T
4 T
5 F

Language Practice p. 13

A
1 signature
2 address
3 name
4 credit card
5 contact number

B
1 c
2 d
3 a
4 b
5 e

Practice More p. 14

A
1 cancel
2 23rd
3 minute
4 canceled

B
1 She called to change her flight.
2 She is going to Tokyo.
3 She is going to leave on June 1.

C
5 → 2 → 3 → 4 → 1

D
1 F
2 F
3 T
4 F

Wrap-Up p. 15

A
1 make a reservation
2 contact number
3 prefer
4 available

5 traveling
6 cash
7 check
8 confirmed
9 flight
10 cooperation

B
1 It's a one-way ticket.
2 It's 680-1403894024.
3 Koreana Air.
4 10:50.
5 1,880 dollars and 90 cents.

Unit 02 May I See Your Ticket and Passport, Please?

Warm-Up p. 16

A
1 baggage tag
2 passport
3 visa
4 kiosk
5 conveyor
6 suitcase

Vocabulary p. 17

1 prohibited
2 baggage claim
3 expiration
4 scale
5 delay
6 check
7 stopover
8 excess
9 carry-on
10 restricted

Listen Up

1 F
2 F
3 T
4 F
5 F

Language Practice p. 21

B
1 F
2 T
3 F

Practice More p. 22

A
1 reservation
2 flight number
3 ready
4 on board

B
1 He is going to London.
2 His passport is not valid.
3 He has to contact his embassy.

128

C
5 → 1 → 2 → 6 → 4 → 3

D
1 F   2 F
3 T   4 F

Wrap-Up   p. 23

A
1 May   2 on time
3 check   4 scale
5 aware   6 through-check
7 weight limit   8 excess
9 need   10 get an upgrade

B
1 They have to put them in their checked luggage.
2 They can carry them in a 1-liter transparent, re-sealable plastic bag.
3 They can carry medication and baby food.

Unit 03 Would You Like a Window or Aisle Seat?

Vocabulary   p. 25
1 cabin   2 Security
3 detector   4 aisle
5 board   6 immigration
7 currency   8 proceed to
9 assignment   10 upstairs

Listen Up
1 T   2 T   3 F
4 F   5 T

Language Practice   p. 27

A
1 on the first floor, across from
2 on the second floor, next to
3 on the first floor, in front of
4 on the first floor, between

B
1 It is going to New York.
2 It departs at 17:30.
3 It leaves from Gate 11.
4 It starts boarding at 17:00.

Language Practice   p. 29

A
1 a   2 e   3 d
4 c   5 b

B
2, 3, 5

Practice More   p. 30

A
1 upstairs   2 turn right
3 first-class   4 end   5 third

B
1 It's going to Paris.
2 Boarding will be delayed for about 30 minutes.
3 It is 11:30.

C
4 → 3 → 2 → 1 → 5

D
1 T   2 F
3 F   4 F

Wrap-Up   p. 31

A
1 aisle   2 emergency
3 carry-on bag   4 take off
5 security bin   6 carry
7 proceed   8 throw away
9 upstairs   10 turn right

B
4 - 2 - 1 - 3

Unit 04 Welcome Aboard!

Vocabulary   p. 33
1 overhead bin   2 devices
3 upright   4 help, with
5 run out of   6 lavatory

7	take off	8	fasten		
9	aboard	10	belongings		

Listen Up
1 F 2 F 3 T
4 F 5 T

Language Practice p. 35
A
1 shut the window shade
2 put your bag in the overhead bin
3 return your seat to the upright position
4 fasten your seatbelt
5 turn off your cell phone
6 remain seated

B
1 T 2 F 3 T
4 F 5 T

Language Practice p. 37
A
1 F 2 F 3 T
4 F

B
1 e 2 c 3 b
4 d 5 a

Practice More p. 38
A
1 fasten 2 pull 3 mind

B
1 The passenger asks to change seats.
2 Yes, he will.
3 They are located in the back of the cabin.

C
5 → 4 → 3 → 1 → 2

D
1 F 2 T 3 F

Wrap-Up p. 39
A
1 fasten 2 takeoff
3 together 4 instead
5 to the right 6 upright position

7	boarding pass	8	with	
9	put	10	have	

B
1 c 2 d 3 a
4 b 5 e

Unit 05 Would You Like Something to Drink?

Warm-up p. 40
A
infant meal, vegetarian meal, Muslim meal

Vocabulary p. 41
1 operates 2 cabin crew
3 on the rocks 4 carry
5 vegetarians 6 accept
7 medicine 8 airsickness
9 change 10 delicious

Listen Up
1 T 2 F 3 F
4 T 5 T

Language Practice p. 43
B
1 e 2 a 3 d
4 f 5 b 6 c

Language Practice p. 45
A
won, United Kingdom, peso, yuan, euro, Japan, Thailand

Practice More p. 46
A
1 Would 2 Place
3 cream 4 extremely

B
1 The cabin crew member wants to know if the passenger has finished his meal.

130

2 The cabin crew member will take away the meal tray.
3 Yes, he did.

C

1 → 5 → 3 → 2 → 4

D

1 F   2 T   3 T

Wrap-Up   p. 47

A

1 something   2 Let
3 carry   4 enjoy
5 Muslim meal   6 duty-free
7 would that be   8 accept
9 finished   10 Place

Unit 06 What's the Purpose of Your Visit?

Warm-up   p. 48

A

1 b   2 c   3 d
4 a   5 e

B

1 c   2 b   3 d
4 a   5 e

Vocabulary   p. 49

1 connect   2 purpose
3 homestay   4 restricted
5 declare   6 customs
7 carousel   8 inspection
9 occupations   10 deplane

Listen Up

1 F   2 F   3 F
4 T   5 F

Language Practice   p. 51

A

1 I'm sorry, but taking photos is not allowed here. (I'm sorry, but you are not allowed to take photos here.)
2 May I have your final destination? (Would you let me know your final destination?)
3 Would you wait behind the yellow line? (Wait behind the yellow line, please.)
4 May I have your occupation? (Would you let me know your occupation?)
5 Would you turn off the electronic devices? (Turn off the electronic devices, please.)

B

1 T   2 F
3 T   4 F

Language Practice   p. 53

A

1 How many   2 How many
3 How many   4 How much
5 How much   6 How many

Practice More   p. 54

A

1 forms   2 index finger
3 look into   4 Hold
5 finished

B

1 The passenger is going to Orlando.
2 No, she didn't.
3 It leaves at 8:30 PM.

C

3 → 4 → 1 → 2 → 5

D

1 F   2 T   3 F

Wrap-Up   p. 55

A

1 arrival   2 purpose
3 long   4 index finger
5 hold   6 declare
7 nothing   8 much
9 exit   10 get to

Answer Key **131**

Unit 07 My Baggage Is Missing

Warm-up p. 56
B
1 baggage claim   2 Internet cafe
3 tax refund counter   4 car rental service
5 customs   6 lost and found
7 bus stop   8 information desk

Vocabulary p. 57
1 conference   2 upset
3 describe   4 deliver
5 fill out   6 trace
7 irregularity   8 property
9 inconvenience   10 official

Listen Up
1 T   2 T   3 T
4 F   5 F

Language Practice p. 61
A
1 b   2 c   3 a
4 e   5 d

Practice More p. 62
A
1 pick up   2 arrive on
3 traveling   4 Carousel

B
1 His baggage has been delayed. (He has not received his baggage yet.)
2 his address and contact number
3 a property irregularity form

C
3 → 2 → 4 → 1

D
1 F   2 T   3 F

Wrap-Up p. 63
A
1 missing   2 baggage claim tag

3 PIR   4 describe
5 regular   6 arrive on
7 inconvenience   8 collect
9 deliver   10 as soon as

Unit 08 I'd Like a Double Room with an Ocean View

Warm Up p. 64
A
1 d   2 g   3 a
B
1 suite   2 twin   3 single

Vocabulary p. 65
1 registration   2 suite
3 concierge   4 receptionists
5 occupied   6 peak
7 disappointing   8 charge
9 rate   10 accommodations

Listen Up
1 F   2 T   3 F
4 T   5 F

Language Practice p. 69
B
1 d   2 f   3 a
4 b   5 e   6 c

Practice More p. 70
A
1 available   2 fully booked
3 peak   4 disappointing

B
1 It's room 206.
2 He asks for a room higher than the 15th floor.
3 He will stay on the 7th floor.

C
4 → 3 → 2 → 5 → 6 → 1

D
1 F   2 T   3 T

Wrap-Up   p. 71
A
1 would   2 charge
3 take   4 change
5 extra bed   6 stay
7 available   8 view
9 occupied   10 fill out

B
1 e   2 c   3 g
4 a   5 f   6 b
7 d

Unit 09 We Have a Business Center on the Second Floor

Vocabulary   p. 73
1 remove   2 faucet
3 complimentary 4 charge
5 equipped   6 request
7 safe   8 apologize
9 clockwise   10 declined

Listen Up
1 F   2 F   3 T
4 F   5 F

Language Practice   p. 75
A
1 I have a problem with the TV. I can't turn it on.
2 I have a problem with the safe. It won't open.
3 I have a problem with the air conditioning. It's not working.
4 I have a problem with the toilet. It won't flush.

Practice More   p. 78
A
1 clockwise   2 complimentary

B
1 It's room 525.
2 He can't turn on the TV.
3 The guest wants to see the Super Bowl.

C
5 → 2 → 1 → 6 → 4 → 3

D
1 T   2 F
3 F   4 T

Wrap-Up   p. 79
A
1 problem with   2 if
3 Turn   4 right away
5 give   6 pay
7 mistake   8 keep
9 reclaim   10 make

Unit 10 What Kinds of Cars Do You Have?

Vocabulary   p. 81
1 vehicle   2 brochure
3 injury   4 mileage
5 brand new   6 insurance
7 performance   8 coverage
9 compact   10 pedestrians

Listen Up
1 F   2 T   3 T
4 F   5 T

Language Practice   p. 83
A
1 What is the rate for three weeks?
2 What is the rental charge for a month?
3 How much is a micro-car for three days?
4 How much is a minivan for five days?
5 How much is an SUV for ten days?

B
1 which   2 who
3 that   4 that
5 that

Answer Key 133

Language Practice
p. 85

A
1. How can I get to Universal Studio?
2. Where is the nearest gas station?
3. Could you tell me how I can get to Tower Bridge?
4. Could you show me the way to the movie theater?
5. Do you know where the Lincoln Memorial is?

B
1. Do Not Enter
2. Right Turn
3. No Right Turn
4. Bike Lane
5. Deer-Crossing Area
6. Falling Rocks
7. Slippery Road
8. Stop
9. No Trucks
10. No Pedestrians

Practice More
p. 86

A
1. type of car
2. minivan
3. available

B
1. He should pay an extra gas charge.
2. It is $3.50 per gallon.
3. Yes, it's higher than the normal pump price.

C
2 → 1 → 4 → 3

D
1. F
2. T
3. T

Wrap-Up
p. 87

A
1. get to
2. fill, up
3. purchase
4. ahead
5. idea
6. comfortable
7. choose
8. rate
9. type
10. miss

Unit 11 Are You Ready to Order?

Vocabulary
p. 89

1. correct
2. rare
3. Ethnic
4. complaint
5. take, order
6. supposed to
7. clam chowder
8. take, out
9. cafeteria
10. spicy

Listen Up
1. T
2. T
3. F
4. F
5. T

Language Practice
p. 91

A
1. Let me tell you about the soup of the day.
2. Let me give you some advice.
3. Let me tell you about my country.
4. Let me check the reservation list.
5. Let me move to another table.
6. Let me introduce myself to you.

Language Practice
p. 93

A
1. This restaurant is too noisy. It's supposed to be quiet.
2. This food is too spicy. It's supposed to be mild.
3. This coffee is too weak. It's supposed to be strong.
4. This soup is too salty. It's supposed to be bland.
5. This movie is too boring. It's supposed to be exciting.
6. This meat is too rare. It's supposed to be medium rare.

B
1. I'm sorry. We don't have any cream of broccoli left, but we do have some minestrone.
2. I'm sorry. We don't have any clam chowder left, but we do have some French onion soup.
3. I'm sorry. We don't have any chocolate pudding left, but we do have some ice cream and a brownie.
4. I'm sorry. We don't have any scrambled eggs left, but we do have some poached eggs and boiled eggs.
5. I'm sorry. We don't have any apple juice left, but we do have some orange juice.
6. I'm sorry. We don't have any salmon filet steak left, but we do have some teriyaki skirt steak.

Practice More
p. 94

A
1 table for three 2 taken
3 try

B
1 It is cooked rare.
2 The guest wants his meat to be cooked medium.
3 The waiter will bring another dish and some water.

C
5 → 4 → 2 → 1 → 3

D
1 F 2 T 3 F

Wrap-Up
p. 95

A
1 reservation 2 table for four
3 show 4 drink
5 have 6 order
7 ready 8 supposed
9 left 10 what

Unit 12 I Need a Present for My Parents

Warm-up
p. 96

B
1 outlet mall 2 supermarket
3 convenience store

Vocabulary
p. 97

1 spend 2 discount
3 refund 4 on sale
5 souvenir 6 bargain
7 exchange 8 receipt
9 gift-wrap 10 fitting room

Listen Up
1 F 2 T 3 F
4 F 5 T

Practice More
p. 102

A
1 189 2 price range
3 bargain 4 fixed
5 look around 6 mind

B
1 They are located on Lincoln Street.
2 It takes five minutes on foot.
3 They close at 8:00 PM.

C
3 → 4 → 1 → 5 → 2

D
1 T 2 F 3 F

Wrap-Up
p. 103

A
1 try on 2 mind
3 off 4 bargain
5 get 6 cash
7 bring 8 wear
9 tag 10 look

Unit 13 I Want to See Some Sights in New York

Warm-up
p. 104

A
1 g (Grand Central Terminal)
2 a (Central Park)
3 c (Times Square)
4 f (Rockefeller Center)
5 b (The Statue of Liberty)
6 e (the Brooklyn Bridge)
7 d (the Empire State Building)

Vocabulary
p. 105

1 depend 2 recommend
3 admission fee 4 allow
5 statues 6 tourist attractions
7 balcony 8 sightseeing
9 include 10 art gallery

Listen Up

1	T	2	F	3	T
4	F	5	F		

Practice More p. 110

A

1	admission	2	twenty dollars
3	twelve	4	change

B

1 She asks him to take a picture.
2 He wants to make them smile.
3 at a tourist attraction

C

3 → 4 → 1 → 6 → 2 → 5

D

1	F	2	T	3	F

Wrap-Up p. 111

A

1	ten-minute walk	2	information
3	sights	4	take
5	whole trip	6	include
7	depends on	8	should
9	located	10	recommend